Heels

to Deals

Heels
to Deals

HOW WOMEN ARE DOMINATING
IN BUSINESS-TO-BUSINESS SALES

Compiled by

HEIDI SOLOMON-ORLICK

Founder and CEO, GirlzWho**Sell**™

BMcTALKS Press
4980 South Alma School Road
Suite 2-493
Chandler, Arizona 85248

Published by BMcTALKS Press, a division of BMcHAWK TALKS LLC, Chandler, Arizona.

Volume pricing is available to bulk orders placed by corporations, associations, and others. For bulk order details and for media inquiries, please contact BMcTALKS Press at info@bmtpress.com or 202.630.1218.

FIRST EDITION
Library of Congress Control Number: 2021924225

ISBN: 978-1-953315-18-2 (paperback)
ISBN: 978-1-953315-19-9 (eBook)

Printed in the United States of America.

DEDICATION

This book is dedicated to all the women in sales who bravely shared their stories and to the women whose stories are still untold. It is dedicated to all the future sales leaders who will take what they have learned and who will continue to carry the torch. And finally, I dedicate this book to my husband, David Orlick, who's unwavering support has allowed me to climb mountains and achieve my wildest dreams. I love you today.

TABLE OF CONTENTS

FOREWORD

Jill Konrath

*Sales Strategist, Speaker,
and Author*

> "A sales career plays to a woman's strengths.
> It's really all about connections, collaboration,
> and preparation."
>
> **– Jill Konrath**

Why in the world would you ever consider a career in sales? After all, it's populated by a bunch of sleezy, manipulative, fast-talking men who care more about their commissions than their customers. That was certainly my impression back when I started selling—and it still holds true for most people today.

The *only* reason I took a sales job was because I had an idea for starting a company and my business advisor said it would fail unless I learned this critical skill. Just a few months later, after getting hired by a major corporation that sells print and digital document products and services, I quickly discovered that everything I believed about sales was totally wrong. Those who succeeded over the long-term truly cared about their customers. These sellers focused on helping prospects and clients achieve their objectives, address business issues, and make good decisions. Later, when I sold technology and professional services, these same types of sellers were always the most successful.

Over time, I started my own consultancy to help companies launch new products and services into the marketplace. Since I love challenges, I also gravitated to emerging sales issues, researching new approaches, and experimenting. Each time I figured out what worked, I wrote a book (*Selling to Big Companies, SNAP Selling, Agile Selling* and *More Sales Less Time*) about the specific topic.

Ultimately, that led to an international speaking career, over one-third of a million followers on a popular online professional networking platform and a massive number of newsletter subscribers. In the past few years, I've been touted as "the fairy godmother of sales"—which always makes me smile—and have been selected a top sales expert by numerous companies and organizations.

But my heart has always been with the women in sales. When I started my career, I desperately needed female role models. After years of complaining that there weren't any and asking, "Why don't they step up?", I realized it was my job to do. So, I did and am proud of what I've accomplished. Women need to see other successful women to realize they can do it.

So, when Heidi reached out to me about her vision for GirlzWhoSell, I wanted to learn more. In our first conversation, she shared her desire to close the gender gap in B2B sales. She also wanted to build the world's largest pipeline of diverse, early-stage, female sales talent. All this was something I could sink my teeth into.

But what really got me was that Heidi was all about motivating women and presenting sales as a viable career option. She no longer wanted women to be accidental salespeople. Instead, she wanted them to choose sales with intentionality. But she also knew that women need to know why sales is a great career option and that, as a female, they already possess many of the most important traits necessary for success. So, in *Heels to Deals*, she's featured the wisdom of many women.

What I love about this co-author collaboration project is the diversity and power of the stories being shared. This book features women from highly diverse backgrounds, ethnicities, race, age, sexual orientation, and career stages. As a reader, you'll find people whose stories you can relate to. You'll also gain invaluable insights and actionable knowledge about what it takes to be successful in this profession.

Personally, I believe that a company's sales team is the heart of their business and a major competitive advantage. No matter how brilliant their product or service, without good salespeople, their business would fail. And women are especially good at delivering stellar results. Research shows they outperform their male counterparts and stay longer in their positions.

If you're even a bit curious about sales, it's time to read *Heels to Deals*. Let me just highlight a few final points: Sales is a lucrative career. It's also challenging, flexible, and lots of fun. But don't just listen to me. After reading all the stories inside, you'll have a good idea if it might be a good option for you. And that will be well worth your time!

Jill Konrath
Sales Strategist, Speaker, and Author
Minneapolis, Minnesota
October 2021

FOREWORD

Lori Richardson
President, Women Sales Pros
Founder, She Sells Summit Boston

In most business sectors, whether you are a rep, a business development representative (BDR), sales development representative (SDR), account executive, manager, vice president, or higher, B2B sales is a male-majority role.

In 2015, I launched Women Sales Pros as a community to help get more women into B2B sales and promote more women into sales leadership. There were no other women in sales groups, communities, or organizations other than for specific industries.

Now we have many communities for women in sales, and one of my favorite ones is GirlzWhoSell led by Heidi Solomon-Orlick. When I first talked with Heidi, I was so impressed by her passion, determination, and focus. Clearly, Heidi is a voice we will be listening to now and into the future.

GirlzWhoSell's mission is "Through training, mentoring, and empowerment, we will develop and build the next generation of B2B sales leaders and change the face of sales."

The time is now to work together—men and women in company leadership and sales leadership. We need to identify more great women for sales roles, and the mission of GirlzWhoSell is to help create a pipeline of early-stage diverse sales talent—something no other women in sales community has really focused on. We need to mentor and sponsor them. Finally, we need to promote women in existing roles into higher levels of sales leadership.

In a pandemic or post-pandemic world, with the opportunity to work remotely or partially remotely, it is the perfect time for company leaders to promote more women into sales roles with increasing responsibility. No one in leadership needs to be a "road warrior" anymore. This attracts more women into executive sales leadership and offers companies more options for top candidates for those roles.

At the same time, we can work together with communities like GirlzWhoSell to educate girls and young women about the amazing careers B2B sales holds.

The stories in this book demonstrate the sort of examples we have in women's journeys in this industry. Read it, recommend it, and buy copies for women who may become inspired to consider a sales career or recommit and rise within the profession we love.

Lori Richardson
President, Women Sales Pros
Founder, She Sells Summit
Boston, Massachusetts
October 2021

LETTER TO THE READER

Samantha McKenna
Award-Winning Sales Leader and Speaker

M y career in sales started with me turning down the first sales job I was offered. Twice. The idea of selling things and inconveniencing people to buy the products I represented was overwhelming in the worst way.

The hiring manager sold me in the end, and it has led to a rocket ship career. Fifteen years in sales, breaking more than thirteen records that still stand, I was the first woman to go from individual contributor (IC) to the executive ranks at one company, to finishing on top as a leader at LinkedIn, to becoming a highly-sought-after keynote speaker, and wrapping a bow on it by launching my own sales consultancy, #samsales. The ultimate test of sales is can you do it yourself when you launch your own business? I'm proud to say that we not only beat our first year's projections by 200%+, but we doubled our previous year's revenue in year two and hit our annual stretch goal in the first six months.

Across my career, I've seen a lot of the good and the bad. But one particular line that a female colleague said to me once was what set me on fire to lift other women in sales. When I asked for help as I onboarded at a new company, she replied, "That's what your boss is for, and I have no interest in seeing you succeed."

What we need is not only more women in sales but more women that lift each other up. We are powerhouses!! Who runs the world? GIRLS. We are process-driven, we are empathetic, we are great question-askers, we are resilient, we remember the big and the small things, we are strategic, and data study after data study shows that women outperform men in sales.

But to get more women here, we need to be the inspiration for other women. We need to invest in them, to rally for them, to share with them, and to celebrate them so that they keep growing, learning, and feeling encouraged to keep going even on the toughest of days. We need to surround ourselves with women who suggest our names when opportunities are present, and we need to BE those women that say the names of others.

I hope this book inspires you to dive head-first into this incredible space of sales or to stay the course if you're already here. There are countless resources from which to learn, this book being one of the first stops on your never-ending journey.

Samantha McKenna
Award-Winning Sales Leader and Speaker
Washington, D.C./Baltimore, Maryland area
September 2021

LETTER TO THE READER

Farnoosh Brock

Published Author, Business Coach, Speaker, and Corporate Trainer

If you've ever dreamt of having your own successful company or playing a big role in one then immediately dreaded the thought of having to sell, we should talk.

My journey started in electrical engineering school followed by coding at a start-up then a twelve-year career at a Fortune 100 tech giant before starting my own company. I excelled at everything as an entrepreneur except one: Selling my services. I hated selling! Why? Because I could not stand the feeling of "being sold to." So how could I do this to my prospects in earnest? It was a real conflict of value and a real dilemma. I had also made myself a promise to never again get a job, so the only way forward was to make my own company work. That is how I became singularly passionate about serving versus selling and began my research on the topic.

Over the years, I proved—in my own business and those of many clients—that when we serve our prospective clients powerfully, when we drop our sales agendas and instead focus on building deep trust, deep connection, and meaningful conversations, we go further in the elusive sales process. We unravel the mystery. We make it more effortless and enjoyable. We stop selling, but we have more sales. Everyone—us, prospects who say "yes," prospects who say "no" or "not yet"—all of us win. My work, *The Serving Mindset: Stop Selling and Grow Your Business*, was published in 2018 and has been the driving force in my overall mission in business. I have had the extreme pleasure of taking this message to the fabulous platform of Talks@Google as well as to Fortune 100 companies, business associations, and leaders who want to change their conversations from selling to serving. Their success only bolsters my confidence that we must set aside traditional selling techniques as a business community. We must put serving and helping people above all else in our business pursuits. And when we adopt the right mindset and strategies to do this well, we experience astronomical success and growth and fulfillment.

That is why I was beyond delighted when I came to learn about Heidi's work on GirlzWhoSell and her genuine approach to selling, which embodies serving. When she asked me to write this letter to you, it was an emphatic "yes" because not only can we—as women, as business owners, as sales executives, and every other profession that requires you to stand up and sell—achieve our sales goal by serving; we can exceed then. We can change the nature of trust in business. We can nurture relationships that come back around with amazing rewards in the future. We can help others be more sincere in their business dealings by being role models. We can be the butterfly effect by changing how we show up, how we serve, and how we achieve our sales goals.

The work that you are about to read is a collection of great wisdom by women who have demonstrated that serving others, building trust, and putting people first can help us sell, sell well, and sell beyond our goals. It is also the change we need to bring to the present and future of business.

Imagine a world where you never made others feel "sold to" but rather one where you cultivated trust, connection, empathy, and even enthusiasm in engaging in sales conversations. Imagine the possibilities where we can create the perfect conditions of business exchange with confidence and sincerity and grow prosperous while being aligned to our values. That is what this work can begin to show you, and I know you will be inspired by GirlzWhoSell.

Farnoosh Brock
Published Author, Business Coach,
Speaker, and Corporate Trainer
Cary, North Carolina
September 2021

10 ACTIONS TO KICKSTART YOUR SALES CAREER

Below are tips and immediate actions you can take to launch your sales career:

1. Identify where you feel powerful right now.
2. Explore what it is that brings you joy, excitement, and personal satisfaction.
3. Complete an honest assessment of your strengths, and identify areas of opportunity, then get additional training if needed! Of course, GirlzWhoSell Academy is always an awesome option.
4. Make a list of brands, companies, and/or products that align with your values; that are committed to diversity, equity and inclusion initiatives; and that are focused on adding women to their sales teams.
5. Update your social media and professional networks.
6. Refresh your résumé with a focus on highlighting your transferable skills and/or relevant sales experience.
7. Join professional organizations like Women Sales Pros, Rev-Women by RevGenius, and the National Association of Women Sales Professionals to name a few.

8. Reach out, connect, and network with women in sales. They want to mentor and help you.

9. Apply for positions even if you don't meet 100% of the listed qualifications.

10. Don't get discouraged. This is a marathon, not a sprint. You are embarking on a journey that will last a lifetime.

DEFINITIONS

Some chapters include abbreviations common in and specific to the world of sales. These definitions have been provided to support a positive reading experience.

ABS: account-based selling

Account-based selling (ABS) is a multi-touch, multi-channel strategy that is coordinated across the entire company to pursue a target number of high-value accounts that have been identified by account-based marketing (ABM). In a collaborative effort, marketing and sales work together to close these accounts.

ABM: account-based marketing

Account-based marketing (ABM) is a focused approach to business-to-business (B2B) marketing in which marketing and sales teams work together to target best-fit accounts and turn them into customers. Also known as key account marketing, ABM is a strategic approach to business marketing that is based on account awareness. The marketing team employs strategies that meld the expertise of sales and marketing to locate, engage with, and close deals with high-value accounts.

B2B: business-to-business

B2B stands for "business to business" and encompasses all companies that create products and services geared toward other businesses. This can include Software-as-a-Service (SaaS) products, B2B marketing firms, and overall business supply companies. B2B companies are supportive enterprises that offer the things other businesses need to operate and grow.

B2C: business-to-consumer

B2C means "business to consumer" and is the type of commerce transaction where businesses sell products or services directly to consumers. Traditionally, this could refer to individuals shopping for clothes for themselves at the mall, dinners eaten in restaurants, or subscribers getting pay-per-view TV at home. More recently, however, the term B2C refers to the online selling of products, or e-tailing, wherein manufacturers or retailers sell their products and services directly to consumers over the Internet.

BDR: business development representative

Business development representatives start conversations with cold leads and are responsible for outbound prospecting and lead generation. They research and reach out to prospective new clients who might be interested in the products and/or services the company sells, educate them on those products and/or services, and introduce those prospects or leads to the company. Business development activities are meant to spot and qualify new opportunities.

CRM: customer relationship management

Customer relationship management (CRM) is a process in which a business tracks its interactions with clients, documenting the stages of moving a client from being a cold prospect to a warm lead to a closed client. The software that businesses use to conduct this tracking is oftentimes referred to as a CRM.

OTE: on-target earnings

On-target or on-track earnings is a term often seen in job advertisements for sales positions, indicating the total pay an employee can expect to receive if she/he reaches a set quota. Because it's based on the employee's performance, the actual pay may be higher or lower than the stated OTE.

PaaS: Platform-as-a-Service

PaaS, or Platform-as-a-Service, is a cloud computing model that provides customers a complete cloud platform—hardware, software, and infrastructure—for developing, running, and managing applications, alleviating customers from having to build and maintain such a platform on-premises.

SaaS: Software-as-a-Service

SaaS is an abbreviation of "Software-as-a-Service" and is a method of software delivery through which end users can access and use an application remotely via Internet browsers. An SaaS vendor houses and maintains the hardware that runs the application.

SDR: sales development representative

Sales development representatives (SDRs) usually engage with warm leads, people who are already considering the company's products and/or services and who may have been approached by a company's business development representative (BDR). SDRs spend their time conducting calls, performing demos, conducting meetings, consulting and problem solving with prospects, convincing potential customers to choose the company, and closing deals. Sales tasks revolve around understanding the prospect's needs and winning them over.

INTRODUCTION

"Becoming" is the Journey

Heidi Solomon-Orlick

Founder and CEO, GirlzWhoSell

Board President, GirlzWhoSell Empowerment Fund

The journey that you are about to embark upon as you read this compilation of stories from some of the most prolific and highly regarded female sales professionals around the world may not be one that you had anticipated. My initial goal of having GirlzWhoSell sponsor a project of this magnitude was to amplify the voices and share the wisdom of diverse women in sales—something that had never been done before. I believe that, as sales is grounded in the foundation of storytelling, the sharing of personal experiences can be transformational. My hope is that this book will inspire the next generation of young women, motivating them to intentionally pursue a career in what I believe to be the best profession in the world, business-to-business sales.

While we certainly exceeded our goal, the book has become so much more than a collection of stories about professional sales. It is about facing truth, celebrating personal triumph, and conquering adversity. It is about making difficult life choices and achieving financial independence while overcoming insurmountable odds. It is about slaying demons, building confidence, letting go of perfection, and realizing that the lot we were given in life does not define us. And finally, it is about friendship, faith, love, and unconditional acceptance.

What I adore most about the stories shared in this book is that it truly demonstrates the power of diversity. While all the featured leaders identify as female, we fall into a wide range of ages, ethnicities, races, career levels, and backgrounds. And yet, despite our differences, there is a cross-section of similarities. Mostly that we all found our way into sales leadership.

It is an age-old question: Are leaders born or are they made? I believe the answer lies somewhere in between: The most successful leaders are "raised."

According to a number of business articles and research by psychologists, including those featured in well-known publications like Forbes.com and *Psychology Today*, the consensus seems to be that, in most cases, leaders are made. We've all heard the saying "she is a natural born leader." But, in fact, the best estimate is that leadership skills are one-third born and two-thirds made. Indeed, some people are born leaders, but for the majority of us, we sit somewhere else on the bell curve.

Humans come into the universe with innate personality traits. Those traits are a roadmap that can lead us down certain paths. Experiences shape and mold these predispositions so that they either grow or dim over time.

Like a flower, these traits need to be nurtured and cared for in order to bloom. A flower requires a solid foundation of soil enriched with nutrients. It needs to be watered, fed, pruned, and loved. Nothing grows without proper nourishment. Our personalities or, as I like to think of it, our sales personality archetypes are very much the same.

Actress and life coach Lisa Haisha has said, "Leaders don't set out to be leaders. They set out to make a difference. It is never about the role—it is always about the goal."

This quote rings true for me. I often say that I didn't choose sales leadership; it chose me. So, regardless of my title or where I am on the hierarchy, there really is no escaping it. If your focus is on solving problems, inspiring others, having an impact, and doing the hard work to achieve and exceed a shared vision or goal, there is a better than average chance that a leadership role will find you whether you are actively looking for it or not.

As a woman in the male-dominated field of professional sales, I have found that some specific pivotal learning moments throughout my life—both the inspiring and the challenging—have made me who I am and have influenced my sales leadership style. Empathy; serving others; overcoming adversity; problem-solving; and my natural curiosity, competitiveness, and compassion have all stemmed from specific life experiences.

Out of these transforming micro-moments, I made some important decisions about who I wanted to be and how I wanted to show up for others. Maybe those traits were always there or maybe they grew over time. I am honestly not sure. What I do know is that it was in these moments that my true sales leadership journey began.

Let me share a few stories that I believe led me to be the leader I am today.

The First Pivotal Moment

I have always been curious about the nature versus nurture debate and frequently questioned whether the environment we are raised in is more or less powerful than the genetics we were born with. You see, I was adopted at five days old. It was a private adoption through an attorney and rabbi. My birth mother was placed in an unwed mother's home as many young, pregnant women were back in 1959.

Immediately following my birth, my mother was forced by her family to give me away despite her wishes to keep me. With the signing of a single piece of paper, I went from Jill Planchak, the name given me by my birth mom, to Heidi Solomon, and the course of my life was forever changed.

From as early as I can remember, I knew that I was wanted, chosen, and definitely loved. I was blessed to be given every opportunity to succeed. In fact, success was a rite of passage. The need to succeed in all aspects of my life was encouraged, emphasized, and rewarded. Perfection was not a nice to have; it was a simple expectation.

While growing up, I was motivated to do the things that came naturally, like competitive sports. Throughout my childhood, I rode horses, trained hard, and ultimately became an alternate in the U.S. Equestrian Team for eventing.

Competitive sports played a big part in my life. Winning and losing was easy to understand. It was black and white: You either won or you didn't. But it was also subjective based on the scoring from the judges. In the end, the results were mostly out of my control. So, instead of obsessing over the outcome, I focused on the process. How I felt about my performance became more important than my score or the ribbon I received. If I got the process right, the end result would take care of itself, and when I fell short, I could adjust, modify, and react to something tangible.

Don't get me wrong—winning mattered. I was highly competitive. But focusing on what was within my control became a way for me to take my power back. I owned the outcome as well as my feelings about the results.

While I had, for the most part, a fortunate childhood, I sensed that certain pieces of the puzzle—my true essence—had evaded me. I couldn't put a finger on it. I was restless, dissatisfied, and sometimes broken. I tried to fill the empty spaces by growing my career, forging casual relationships, and finally getting married and having children. My life was full, yet I still felt something was missing.

It wasn't until my early forties, when I tried to find out some genetic information about my son's hearing impairment that I had the opportunity to meet both of my birth parents. At that moment, I realized that there were sides of my personality that had not yet been fully developed or explored. My artistic predisposition; my propensity to lead; and my desire to serve, give back, and make the world a better place than how I found it were not only learned but were a part of my DNA. For the first time, I embraced the desire to move beyond materialism and transcend into a life motivated by a spiritual calling that was bigger than myself. I brought the yin and the yang of being together to form one—like two sides of a single coin. For the first time in my life, I felt whole. I was truly happy and prepared to make a lasting impact in the world of sales. My career took off, and I have never looked back.

The Second Pivotal Moment

As a young child, I was boundless. I never wanted to color within the lines. In fact, I was defiant because it felt restrictive, confining, like a racehorse being held back by the reins. Conversely, by nature, I was also a people pleaser and a rule follower. I thrived on recognition and wanted to be accepted. I needed that gold star. As I got older, I feared pushing the boundaries because I would get scolded.

In my generation, boundary-busting was not encouraged, especially from young women. We were told to be "good girls," seen and not heard, sugar and spice and everything nice until we weren't, which was most of the time for me.

Over time, I succumbed to the linear universe to which so many children are subjected: the black and white box of right and wrong, good and bad ... the world of standardized tests and the need to conform. As singer, songwriter, and political activist Malvina Reynolds put it, "boxes, little boxes, little boxes all the same."

The problem for me was that I did not see the world in black and white. I not only felt comfortable in the gray, but I wanted to live in a world of color—orange and purple and blue ... a world where rainbows were the norm and colors could be mixed together to make more exquisite shades ... a world where all colors were considered beautiful and accepted. Today, this is called diversity, equity, and inclusion. But, as we all know way too well, in the real world, that dream is not always possible.

So, I asked "why" a lot. And when the answer didn't make sense or didn't come at all, I asked why some more ... until middle school.

Starting in seventh grade, your intelligence is defined based on the results of an IQ test. I recall taking the IQ test for the very first and last time. It did not make sense to me. My brain was not wired in the way that the test wanted me to think. At the time, I clearly did not recognize its significance or the long-term impact of the results. On a rainy Monday, my mom and I were called into the principal's office. The results were in. The atmosphere was grim as though someone had died. The principal did a read-out of the results. The scores were low. I mean really low.

My mom looked confused. She asked, "If the results are so low, how can my daughter be doing so well in school?" I remember the reply as clear today as the day it happened. The principal exclaimed, "Don't worry, Mrs. Solomon. Your daughter may not be smart, but she works harder than any student I know. She puts in the extra effort, and if she keeps doing that, she will find a way to succeed in her life."

The world stopped. Everything I knew to be true about myself had, in a single moment, been stripped away. That day, I made a decision. I was not going to be categorized. I was not going to be measured in comparison to the norm because the norm was average, and average was not my life's goal. The test did not define me; it was just a small part of the whole.

But give 100%, I certainly did. In middle school I organized a school protest to fight for a girl's equal right to wear pants and won. I played football on the girls' "recreational" team over being a cheerleader, and I studied hard. And while it may have taken me longer to complete an assignment, overall, I did pretty well in school. I wasn't a straight-A student, but I had a full life and was well-rounded. And I made it my life's mission to prove the system wrong, to challenge the status quo, and to defy the odds. I would succeed not in spite of the system but because of it.

Over time, I began to realize that intelligence can be quantified in many different ways. IQ is one measurement, but perhaps more important, especially in sales leadership, is EQ, or emotional intelligence. EQ is most often defined as the ability to perceive, use, understand, manage, and handle emotions. EQ is my superpower.

The Third Pivotal Moment

I often get asked about how I entered into the field of professional sales. I want to share a little secret. Trust me when I tell you that when I was a young adult and was asked what I wanted to be when I grew up, a woman in business-to-business tech sales was not even in my top 50 of what I imagined myself doing. At one point I wanted to be a dancer, then a professional athlete, and then, after college, a journalist. I imagined myself working for a national magazine known for its stunning images and its distinctive thick square-bound glossy format with a yellow rectangular border, traveling around the world reporting on the extinction of habitats or reporting for a popular New York-based American business-focused, international daily newspaper, interviewing world leaders. So, what was the "aha" moment when I knew sales might be right for me? It was about proving someone wrong. You see...

My dad was the best sales guy I knew, but he actually discouraged me from pursuing a career in it. In fact, in college, when I asked if he would train me to take over his company when I graduated, he told me that there was no way a woman could survive—let alone sell—in the textured coating business. Sales was a man's job. Not a totally unusual mindset for someone born in 1928, so I do forgive him. But you can imagine that comment lit a fire in my belly! Ultimately, my father handed over his business to my younger brother and a few "trusted" male partners who eventually drove the company into bankruptcy.

Now, I am no therapist but there is likely no surprise that after the "rejection" from my father, I was on a mission to prove to the world that women could be great at sales, particularly in traditionally male-dominated industry sectors. If he wouldn't let me sell for him, I would certainly sell for others. The rest, as they say, is history.

The Final Pivotal Moment

While we are on the topic of my father, I want to share this last important moment. Besides being a highly successful entrepreneur, the greatest salesman on earth, and an angel with the patience of a saint and a heart the size of the ocean, my dad was an incredible storyteller.

When I was a young child, he would tuck me into bed at night. Each night he would make up these fantastic stories about Mumbo, Jumbo, and Dumbo, a family of three elephants who would embark on daily adventures together.

Dumbo, the baby, was particularly mischievous and was always getting herself into trouble. She was curious, courageous, and competitive. And while those were great traits, they sometimes led her down the wrong path.

Each story was based on a place my father or our family had traveled, a tough situation we had found ourselves in, or a problem we would have to solve for. Dad and I would talk about the challenge, and he would ask, "If you were Dumbo, what are some things that you could do to get yourself out of this mess?"

And together, we would come up with solutions.

Of course, Dumbo was quite the clever little elephant, and she would always find her way coming out the other side a little smarter, a little braver, and a little more confident. By the end of the story, Dumbo would resolve the problem, and the family would be at peace, ready to face whatever challenge the next day might bring.

Does this sound like sales to you? It does to me.

These pivotal moments taught me the values that I carry with me today. They are the basis for how I lead and how I interact with clients and are the foundation of my life. But you may be asking what does all this mean and how do these stories connect back to sales leadership?

Let me leave you with a few thoughts:

- Embrace diversity. Teams from diverse backgrounds sharing different perspectives are exponentially more successful. It is our duty as leaders to recognize, respect, and nurture the uniqueness of every human being.
- Life is not black and white, it is not linear, and it certainly is not perfect. Sometimes it is messy. The ability to live, be comfortable in, and manage through the gray is important.
- Respect different perspectives and opinions. Every person on a team looks at and solves problems differently, which is a great

advantage. There is not only one right answer, and there are no bad ideas.

- Recognize beauty when you see it. It is the range of colors that makes a rainbow complete.
- Seek out employees who are not a reflection of you but those who represent the broad spectrum of your customers. Confront inherent bias, and question intentions when choosing same over different. It is this awareness that allows us to grow as people and as leaders.
- Think expansively. Each person comes to your team with their own story and unique set of circumstances. It is the team's collective life experiences that allow each individual within the team to succeed. The combined strength of the group will counterbalance our individual weaknesses. Like pieces to a puzzle, only together are we whole.
- Process matters. What gets measured gets managed.
- Be honest. Remember, people not only buy from people they like but from people they trust.
- Be empathetic. Instead of criticizing, seek to understand. Listen actively and deeply. It is through listening that we find truth.
- Winning is important, but it isn't everything. Learn from the losses.
- Hard work supersedes all other measurements of success.
- Be curious. Ask "why," and never accept "because I said so" as an answer. If there is no answer, find one.
- Serve others before yourself. Leadership is not about the leader; it is about what the leader brings to the team.

I want to end with a quote from the great Dr. Seuss in my favorite sales leadership book *Oh, The Places You'll Go!*

"So be sure when you step, step with care and great tact. And remember, life is a Great Balancing Act. And will you succeed?

Yes! You will indeed (98 and ¾ percent guaranteed). Kid, you'll move mountains!"

We *are* the sum of our environment combined with our genetic roadmap. What we do with this knowledge will define and influence the sales leaders we become. "Becoming" is the journey. The final destination is up to us.

SET NEW STANDARDS OF PERFORMANCE

Alice Kemper
President

What was your path to the sales industry?

My mother will tell you I knew I wanted to be a schoolteacher from the moment I could talk. Beginning at two years old, you would find me playing "school" for endless hours in the basement with my dolls and the ones I confiscated from my older sister.

I did teach in the public school system for three years and even began a master's in education graduate program to earn my degree to become a principal.

Although teaching was my passion, during the three years I was teaching, it was without a contract because of contract negotiation issues between the teachers and the school board, and I was earning the same as year one with no raises in sight.

Sadly, a teacher's salary couldn't provide the finances to do the three most basic things: (1) pay my living expenses; (2) have spending money; and most importantly, do what my father impressed upon me ... (3) save. I could do two of the three—not all three—and all three were important goals of mine.

Thus, I knew it was time for a new career, and I wanted one where I didn't need to go back to school for a law or nursing degree.

It was 1976, and a good friend was home on the tennis courts at 3:30 p.m. every day. I was curious as to what job allows you a good income and your day can end at 3:30. Turns out, he was in liquor sales, and I decided I wanted a sales job like that!

At the time, women were primarily only in pharmaceutical or cosmetic sales. I knew I didn't want to go around to doctors' offices dropping off samples, and my interview with a multinational cosmetics, skin care, fragrance, and personal care company ended after the first cosmetic question—possibly as simple as "What mascara do you use?" as I was a no make-up kind of gal at the time and had no clue about make-up, especially since my girlfriends were the ones who dressed and made me up for the interview.

I kept looking in the classified ads, and a major greeting card company had an open sales position in Tampa, Florida. Unknown to me at the time, the company had asked the hiring managers to consider hiring a woman as they needed to meet Equal Employment Opportunity Commission requirements.

And for that, I am forever grateful to Bernie Martinez who believed in me with no sales background and hired me. Later, I found out there was plenty of whispering going on with the other twelve male sales reps in the district about how and what I, as a woman, must have done to get hired. It also turned out I was the eleventh woman hired in a nationwide sales team of 870.

Knowing I was a token—and very proud of it!—I was determined to show them women are a force to be reckoned with. This fueled me to never stop striving to not only meet goals but to exceed them. I knew I had to sell better than any of the men and set new standards of performance.

Although the company had an excellent two-week classroom on-boarding sales training program at headquarters, I committed to learning as much as I could on my own about the art of selling

I became a voracious reader and questioned anyone I met who was in sales. Listening, applying, and adapting to become a strategic business partner with everyone I was selling and servicing became my mantra.

Relying on others to train and mentor me was not an option. I alone needed to take charge of my success.

It worked. I exceeded my sales quota, and within two years of excelling in the Tampa sales market, I was promoted to assistant sales manager of the Miami, Florida district.

My responsibility as assistant sales manager was to ride in the field Monday through Thursday, training and coaching all twenty-two sales reps.

They were all older and more experienced than I, and did I mention they were all men? Rumor had it that they also thought I slept my way into that position. Now, I turned my listening skills and sales skills around as these men were my new clients. By following the same sales steps to coaching, I was accepted, and the learning became a two-way opportunity.

In retrospect, everything I learned as a sales representative and assistant sales manager aided in my success in every sales leadership position and as a founder of a sales training solution firm.

Two years later, sexism reared its ugly head with that greeting card company, and the writing on the wall indicated, as a woman, my career advancement days were over.

I went in search of the next company to value my sales and sales leadership skills even though I was told by recruiters I would never land a sales manager position without starting in sales at the new company.

Once again, I was on a mission to prove them wrong. The recruiters did have it wrong. The product is the easy part to learn. My years of sales and sales leadership were the hard part to learn, and I had already excelled in that. I knew I didn't have to work my way up from sales to sales leadership. Once again, I learned not to allow others' limited beliefs to stifle mine.

Harte Hanks Communications, under the tutelage of Dick Mandt—and thank you, Dick—came my way. The opportunity was for a start-up with two inside and six outside reps. I jumped on it, and within three years, built an inside sales team of twenty-two to a full call center and an outside sales team of thirty-three. Then Harte Hanks asked me to turn around a business unit in Tucson, Arizona, and off I went. After a year in Tucson with a verbally abusive boss, I took the cue from the friends who were calling and asking me to help with their sales teams.

In 1983, I launched Sales Training Consultants. With the help of my team of sales trainers, we have since delivered 2,200 plus workshops to more than 66,500 sales representatives worldwide with our clients boasting 5% to 35% sales and productivity increases in ten short weeks. Fast forward, my book title was always going to be *52 Sixty-Minute Sales Meetings* until sales managers told me they would only give up thirty minutes max for sales meetings! At first, I thought "How could I possibly create high-impact, high-payoff sales training meetings in just thirty minutes?" yet I took the challenge. In 2009, I began selling our done-for-you 30-Minute Sales Meetings using our unique 3E Sales Accelerator Method to sales managers worldwide in an online digital marketing membership site.

What motivated you to be in sales versus any other career?

Reflecting, my experience selling for that greeting card company launched my career and my love of selling. At the time, I also thought I had died and gone to heaven on my very first day of work because I more than doubled my income as my base salary was twice as much as my teaching salary, plus I was given a company car with gas, an expense account, and potential for commissions to triple my teaching salary income.

Here I was pursuing my passion for teaching, taking courses to obtain my master's in education to become a principal, and at the same time being hindered in my earning potential as an educator.

It was time to find a new profession where I could earn more money to meet my personal financial goals.

My list of professions with higher earnings—nurse, lawyer, financial planner—all required another degree, which wasn't appealing and not really an option to go to school fulltime without an income.

I even asked my father if I could join him in the family business, the largest remodeling company in Baltimore, and the answer was a flat-out "No, girls don't do that." Yet, after my successful career in sales and sales leadership, Dad tried for years to get me to join the family business.

Typical of me, I was not going to let that stop me, and I noticed my friend, Jay, living a good life, showing up on the tennis courts every day at 3:30 p.m. I set out to find out all about his job as a liquor sales rep and then set my sights on a job in sales.

I gave up teaching and signed on with a staffing company that placed temporary secretaries with a variety of companies that needed temporary replacements—either their secretary was going on vacation, was out for medical leave, or had quit and left them in a bind.

Making this change without having secured a sales position was an ethical decision because I didn't want to begin a school year with my students, find my next dream job, and need to leave the students in the middle of the school year. Change is difficult for youngsters, and their mental stability was important to me.

As part of my strategy to find a job in sales without any experience, being placed in a variety of companies around town became one tactic in my networking plan. There were several companies who turned into contacts for me—only I couldn't get excited to sell nuts and bolts or tires.

While working for the staffing company, I continued to scour the classifieds for opportunities until that major greeting card company hired me as a sales representative.

What is one or more myths or negative perceptions about sales or women in sales that need dispelling?

Two myths that stand out and I hoped that, by now, would not remain are as follows:

- Men are better at selling and negotiating.
- Women with kids will have trouble meeting their business responsibilities.

Why do these even exist?

In my experience, these myths show up in companies whose sales teams have 80 to 90% men, and the leadership teams are 95% men. Companies that have more diversity are less likely to maintain these beliefs because they've had positive experiences with the women they hire.

Companies that still adhere to those myths do not value women, and not only do these companies not seek out women, but women probably also wouldn't want to work for them either. These companies are the ones losing out on exceptional talent.

The good news is there are companies that don't hold these or other myths, and my advice to women is don't believe any of these myths; create your own future, and find organizations that value people and show that their values match yours.

What advice would you give to a young woman (or your 19-year-old self) who is considering a career in sales? What can anyone of any age do right now to prepare for a career in sales?

My advice to young women who are considering a career in sales is as follows:

1. Believe in yourself. Don't let anyone who says "you can't, you shouldn't, that's not for you, why would you want that" stand in your way. Be a "duck," and let those comments run off your back and not stick in your head or your energy. There are often more people who are not risk-takers, who are negative, and see the world through their lens and not yours, and they try to pawn their stuff off on you. Don't let them. Evaluate if these people are good for you or not. If not, fire them as friends and advisors. Stick to your passion and what you know is right for you. You've got this!

2. Seek out a mentor now. Women do love to help, guide, and develop other women. Find one who will do that with and for you. You may even want to "intern" for your mentor, work on her projects, her paperwork, and other aspects of the job, and work on your learning curve now.

3. Keep a journal. When you hear a good sales question or observe someone who has you finding yourself saying or thinking,

"They are good," capture what they did that caused you to have that reaction. When you read an article on sales or selling that resonates with you, write it down or put the paragraph or article in your journal.

4. Follow successful women in sales on social media. I continuously join groups, and often some are appalling in how they answer sales help questions; I stay in those groups to remind me how *not* to sell. Making connections now will help when you begin the interviewing process.

Biography

As President of Sales Training Werks and Sales Training Consultants, Alice and her team consistently provide sales organizations the tools to drive sales 5% to 35%, improve employee retention, hire right the first time, and build leaders within the organization.

Alice also excels at designing high-impact, high-payoff thirty-minute or less sales training meeting outlines with her unique 3E Sales Accelerator Method for time-deprived sales managers who know training and coaching their sales team is paramount to success.

Prior to Alice's founding Sales Training Consultants in 1983 and Sales Training Werks in 2009, she led outside sales teams and call centers while simultaneously growing her career in sales and working as an educator in the public school system.

When Alice isn't coaching, facilitating, or writing workshops, you'll find her honing her golf game, making jewelry, birding, or hiking with her long-time significant other.

CONVERT CONVERSATIONS INTO CURRENCY

Precious Williams
CEO

What was your path to the sales industry?

Sales! Sales! Sales! I came to sales when I realized that being an attorney was no longer an option for me. I wanted to create my own company and have the ability to write my own paycheck. But how do I start? Who would believe in a woman with no MBA or demonstrated experienced sales skills? I believed in myself, yet was that enough? Heck yes!!!

My journey into sales began when I fell in love with a man who saw me as beautiful despite me being 327 pounds. I had recently left my ex-fiancé and was sort of lost—unsure of myself. Unsure of myself. However, I put an ad on a dating website and wrote a poem called "Two to Tango!" I never dreamed that the man of my dreams would appear and yet he did! That pitch and poem was everything and was setting me up for the stellar sales career I now have as the #KillerPitchMaster.

The love of my life was a famous actor, and he wanted to show me off. He held my hand in public and flew me out to see him on set! What??? A big girl's dream came true! For the first time in my life, I started to see myself as he saw me. Beautiful. Noticed. Wanted. Loved. I felt called to start my first business, Curvy Girlz Lingerie, the ultimate shopping experience for full-figured divas and plus-size fashionistas. The only problem was that people around me told me to stay with my day job. There was absolutely no way that a fat Black woman without an ivy league degree would have a chance in business with no connections or media interest.

In fact, who cares about curvy women? I did and still do! I cared because I knew we mattered, and no one created red hot, sexy, and fresh lingerie for us. So, being ever the trailblazer, I started my company with nothing but research, a hope, and a dream. But how did I learn to sell? I learned through the art of pitching. I went to an event I could not afford and managed to pitch my business—the one that neither my family nor my friends believed in—and afterwards, they offered me to be featured on the "Elevator Pitch" segment of J.J. Ramber's MSNBC show, "Your Business." When I actually appeared on the show, I walked away with $500,000! So, my first two pitches knocked it out of the park with the producers and investors!

I then entered fourteen business elevator pitch competitions and became a thirteen-time national champion. Pitching is selling! Once I sold my idea and dream of Curvy Girlz Lingerie to investors, I was bitten by the sales bug. It led me to start my second business, Perfect Pitches by Precious, where I am hired by Top Fortune 500 companies to work with and create a sales program and scripts for the sales teams!!! Sales is in my blood, and now I won't let it go!

What motivated you to be in sales versus any other career?

I was motivated to choose sales over other professions because I am really good at it. I did not know that before. In fact, I stayed away from sales positions when I was younger because I thought I had no talent at it. The thing is when I believe in the product or service, I am a sales pitch master! Sales offered me the opportunity to provide unique value to big companies, corporations, foundations, and nonprofits as well as entrepreneurs and speakers.

Before I became a serial entrepreneur, I thought sales were so hard. However, when I started my first two companies and was successful, I knew I still needed to invest in myself and my skillset to keep it fresh. I didn't know that when I started, I would become a three-time #1 bestselling author, a sought-after corporate sales trainer, and an international professional speaker. These are all bonuses. I have the ability to write my own paychecks based on my talents and skills. Who would not want to be in sales?

Sales is the lifeblood of any business or enterprise. If you can demonstrate the ability to sell, there really are no limits! You will be blessed with opportunities that no one else gets. You become a sales queen, and the world truly smiles on you. Because so many people fear sales and do not develop the skills necessary, their lack of confidence makes it easy for me to walk right in and close the deal.

There are many aspects to sales that most do not know. The ability to read a room, size up your prospect, bait, attract, and close with ease all sound easy, yet they are not. With repetition, sales coaching, and mastery, you will be blessed with opportunities no one else receives. You can help a business turn the corner after tragedy; your sales can spur on new products and services and make you the go-to expert in your field. Own your zone of genius in sales!

What an awesome profession!

What is one or more myths or negative perceptions about sales or women in sales that need dispelling?

A few myths about selling are that ...

- Girls and women cannot sell as well as men—That's not true even a little bit!
- You are either born with sales skills, or you can never learn sales—Not true at all. Sales skills can be learned
- Sales is so hard that only very few can do it—Not true. With proper training and confidence, you can do this!
- If you are a salesperson, your job is to force people to buy your products or services—Not true. People hate to be sold to but love to buy. Give them great reasons why, qualify your leads, and make sure what you offer is right for that audience and the difficulty goes down a lot!
- As a salesperson, getting objections is a bad sign—It's actually a good sign because they are listening and have questions. Answer with confidence.
- Most salespeople have no integrity or morals—Not true. Great salespeople have integrity and won't sell anything they do not believe in—PERIOD!
- Most salespeople will sell anything for a buck—Not true. As previously indicated, I cannot sell something I do not like, do not think works, or is a waste of time.
- Most salespeople are cold and are only about the money—Not true. Salespeople want to make their sales goals but also want repeat clients. It's in our best interest to have satisfied clients again and again!

What advice would you give to a young woman (or your 19-year-old self) who is considering a career in sales? What can anyone of any age do right now to prepare for a career in sales?

I want you to be a bad chick with a power sales pitch—PERIOD!!! Do you want to know where the money resides? In SALES!!!!

My advice for a young woman considering a career in sales is that you only live once—try sales! You just might like it! You might create your own business or help another business explode its growth and expand. The world is your oyster as a successful saleswoman!

Most young women shy away from the challenge and promise of sales—just like I once did. Had I taken advantage of sales before, I could have had better clients as an attorney, a great book of business, and made partner faster.

I have since learned that once you master it and add your own funk, you are unstoppable. If you can sell, companies, corporations, nonprofits, etcetera will seek you out. There are several organizations to help you, so check them out!

For those of us at any age, I advise you to prepare for a career in sales by ...

- Seeking out a great sales opportunity.
- Investing in sales training.
- Researching your prospects and target market.
- Going deeper; this is where the money resides.
- Measuring your progress and achievements in sales.
- Keeping notes on your improvements.
- Considering getting a sales coach as you start to see traction.
- Helping another young woman see the value in sales.
- Humble bragging and bringing on Your Inner Beyoncé.
- Tooting your own horn.
- Challenging yourself.

Biography

Every time you open your mouth, your prospects will be throwing money at you. Learn the simple steps to wowing your customer with a perfect pitch with Precious L. Williams the #KillerPitch Master.

Convert conversations into currency. Get the tools and tenacity to pitch with power, sell with storytelling, and develop a masterful mindset for communication. It's time for you to learn how to #SlayAllCompetition

Precious busts norms and shifts perspectives to help teams own their awesome and bring out their "wow" factor. Your leaders and teams will up their game—on their terms—in order to develop the cunning, clarity, and confidence that's been inside them all along.

What's more, they'll get unstuck and discover a renewed and refreshed energy to own the mindset of the pitch in a way they never thought possible. If you're ready to go from milquetoast to memorable, attracting and captivating your prospects while closing the sale in an authentic way, it's time to #pitchforprofit

And you can bet you're going to have fun doing it!

Precious L. Williams is a thirteen-time national elevator pitch champion. She has also been featured on "Shark Tank;" CNN; *Wall Street Journal*, *Forbes Magazine*; *Black Enterprise Magazine*, *Essence Magazine*; and the movie, *LEAP*. Her current clients include Microsoft, LinkedIn, Google, NBCUniversal, Federal Reserve Bank, Intuit QuickBooks, Harvard University, and more. Precious is a dynamic speaker, effective trainer and three-time #1 bestselling author.

TRY TO GENUINELY HELP OTHERS

Stella Ikhnana

Customer Education Consultant

What was your path to the sales industry?

Growing up, I always had something to say. I moved my hands as if I was conducting an orchestra and was always told "You are so expressive when you talk!" I would respond with "Thank you!" each and every time I was given that feedback.

Immigrating to the US from Iraq when I was six, I immersed myself in learning the English language and relied on my teachers to teach me not only grammar and syntax but also social norms and customs. As I thought about what I wanted to be when I was older, I knew it had to be a profession where I help people achieve a goal.

I enrolled in Loyola University Chicago as a special education undergraduate student. My love of education and experiences as a student led me to, hopefully, become that teacher for at least one other student. I taught for ten years, always enrolling in professional development workshops to learn about the newest and best teaching practices. I earned my master's degree as a reading specialist since I saw the biggest challenge for students across the board was their inability to read with fluency and comprehension.

I wanted to infuse all of the new practices into my lessons and was eager to share my knowledge with my colleagues. Unfortunately, throughout my ten years, the educational system became something I didn't sign up for, prioritizing assessments and seeing learners as "data points" more than people.

I knew it was time to pivot, and I explored my options. Several people said to try out sales since I had experience for ten years "selling education" to the most reluctant audience, eleven- to thirteen-year-olds. I was hesitant to enter the sales field. I thought my day-to-day would consist of cold calling hundreds of people, resulting in hundreds of people on the other end sharing their dislike of me reaching out, followed by hanging up on me.

When I began diving into learning more about the sales industry, I saw the direct connection to my passion of helping people achieve a goal. I knew finding the right fit company would be key, a mission-driven company that designed a software or a program to help professionals and/or learners of any age achieve a goal.

What motivated you to be in sales versus any other career?

As a former Special Education Teacher transitioning to sales, I want to continue to prioritize people and provide them with paths to successfully reach their goals. Regardless of their goals, most people can agree they want to work smarter, not harder. I want to ensure that with each and every interaction with clients, I lead with empathy, active listening, and emotional intelligence.

I want to bring the human connection and humor to sales. Based on my experiences, too much outreach is the dreaded automated messages. I want to be part of the future of sales, which is full of relationship building and personalized messages.

Nowadays, every company has tons of competition, several other products offering the exact same solution to a problem but with a small tweak or difference. The biggest factor in standing out from the competition is to lead with kindness and transparency. In my experience, it's best to ask clients "What is your biggest challenge or goal?" then provide facts on how your program might be able to help them achieve their goal and end the conversation by reminding them they are in charge, that they have the option to continue on their current path or try out a free trial to see if another program can help them achieve their goal more efficiently and effectively. This type of approach is one path the sales industry can utilize to be on the right side of the ever-changing and competitive market.

What is one or more myths or negative perceptions about sales or women in sales that need dispelling?

The biggest misconception of sales is individuals say or do whatever to land a sale. It might be the way some in sales go about achieving their goals, but that is not the approach of everyone. I've met countless sales professionals—many who value transparency, building a positive rapport with clients, and trying to genuinely help others achieve their professional goals.

In my opinion, sales is about ensuring the product is truly what the client needs, not just a sale for the sake of a sale. When there's a direct connection of the client to the product, it can lead to forever champions of the product.

What advice would you give to a young woman (or your 19-year-old self) who is considering a career in sales? What can anyone of any age do right now to prepare for a career in sales?

The best video I have seen as a professional is Alan McCarthy's "The 10 Rules of Negotiation." Within this video, you learn the most important skills that can apply to sales, job seeking, or any industry. Alan's negotiation rules are as follows:

1. Don't negotiate.
2. Don't negotiate with yourself.
3. Never accept the first offer.
4. Never make the first offer.
5. Listen more and talk less.
6. No free gifts.
7. Watch out for the "salami" effect.
8. Avoid the rookie's regret.
9. Never make a quick deal.
10. Never disclose your bottom line.

Thank you, Michi Hu Pezeshki, for sharing this video with me and the Recast Success cohort.

Biography

Ever since I was young, I loved going to school, actively partici-pating in class, and completing my work on-time. When I became a Special Education Teacher, I felt comfort in knowing I would continue to be in the school setting, and my goal was to spark the love of education for all learners!

For ten years, I loved working with students of all ability levels and creating activities that sparked their interests, got them talking, and excited to learn.

I learned to be patient and hopeful by observing their perseverance through unimaginable events whether it related to their academic and/or personal struggles. I was in awe how eleven- to thirteen-year-olds could muster up the strength to push forward and move on, taking on each day as a fresh new start.

They inspired me to push forward and move on, to come to school when I was exhausted, burned out, and didn't have the "first day of school" energy. This year would have been my eleventh year of teaching, but I am no longer there.

I've started a new journey, taking my experiences and infusing them into sales and customer education consulting. I'm thankful to have met Heidi Solomon-Orlick, the compiler of *Heels to Deals*, during my journey. Thank you, Heidi, for your efforts in celebrating women in sales! You are an inspiration to me!!

FEAR—FACE EVERYTHING AND RISE

Shawanda Roberts
Vice President of Sales

What was your path to the sales industry?

My first job was in the telemarketing industry at the age of sixteen. My introduction to sales began with selling die cast models to avid motorcycle collectors of a certain popular Milwaukee-based brand. During college, I was an intern at a car rental agency where the only selling component was selling customers car insurance on the vehicle they rented. After graduation, I worked at a Fortune 100 financial services company selling and servicing consumer loans and scheduling financial planning appointments for certified financial planners.

A few years later, a friend recommended me for a business development role within the consulting industry. This is when I started to realize that sales wasn't something that I liked but something that I loved. This was my first exposure to B2B selling, and it forced me to think about the sales industry in a different light. I was working with the investment community, helping them understand markets that they wanted to invest millions of dollars into. It was a complete change from the B2C sales that I was used to. I learned consultative selling and how to prospect and cold call on a whole new level. I had to learn what personas were and how to ask the right questions to pique their interest.

I walked in knowing zero about the investment community nor did I know what market research or strategy consulting was! I remember talking to my mom who told me to hurry up and get on the other side of FEAR—Face Everything and Rise—because I had this in the bag! I took on the challenge and went above and beyond to study the industry and understand the clientele and how they used this type of research and advisory work in their strategy. My mom was absolutely right because within a short amount of time, I was one of the top salespeople not only in my division but in the Americas region. I was asked by management to take on more responsibilities including leading the team. This included managing some of the very same people who had trained me when I first came into the company.

This was the beginning of my journey in a player/coach role. I still held my individual contributor target, but I now had a team target to hit based on the sales executives that were under my purview. I was soon promoted to director, and shortly thereafter, moved into a vice president role. Throughout my journey, I had the opportunity to take on new tasks by corporate including investor presentations and helping to come up with our inaugural Business

Development Executive (BDE) Academy, managing a class of BDEs that came into the organization. It was and still is an honor to manage and be there for the same colleagues who were there for me as I was gaining the knowledge and experience of the role.

What motivated you to be in sales versus any other career?

I love building relationships and helping people solve problems. I have always been this energetic, bubbly, and social person so having random conversations with complete strangers and learning more about them came natural to me. I must admit that if my friend had not recommended going into B2B sales more than fifteen years ago, I am not sure I would have found the LOVE for sales like I have now. The saying is true that God puts people and opportunities in your path all the time. It is up to you to seize the right opportunities. I am forever grateful to my friend for making the recommendation to get into B2B sales.

Sales gives me the opportunity to have a flexible schedule, but in order to truly thrive and have success, you must have a strict discipline in managing your time and not get to the point in which you are abusing that freedom. Abusing that flexibility and not working effectively will quickly lead to the obvious: not hitting quotas and revenue targets, which will surely be one of the quickest ways to get fired from a sales job. Having flexibility helps you truly own your day and schedule. As a mother of three children, this is invaluable. I can be there to pick up the kids when needed, go to appointments, and much more while still doing my work and meeting my deadlines.

When I started my first B2B sales job, I remember talking to my boss and asking her what my schedule was going to be. I wanted to know exactly what time I needed to be there and leave for the day and how much time I got for lunch. I was shocked and thought

I was dreaming when she gave me the answer. She said, "You can come in between 8:30 a.m. and 9:00 a.m., and for lunch, we take about an hour or so." Now coming from a phone sales job where I had to clock in and out for every stinking break or for any reason I needed to be off the phone, this was absolute freedom to me! I remember asking several times the same question to make sure that I was hearing her correctly. She probably thought I was a lunatic that could not comprehend easily. One thing about working in a call center environment is that it taught me discipline, so having the freedom of going and coming as I wanted did not overwhelm me. If I did not have this discipline prior to joining the firm, I would have most likely abused this benefit.

The sales industry allows me to have unlimited income based solely on me and how hard I work. The industry offers multiple compensation options from commission only to base salary only to everything in between. Our commissions were uncapped, meaning there was no limit to how much I could make by selling my organization's products and services year after year. This was a huge motivation for me as I could raise my own goals higher and higher every year regardless of the target I was given. This benefit alone pushed me to establish new relationships with new accounts while expanding on existing relationships within my book of business. These relationships turned into not only business but weaved into personal relationships that I could always take with me wherever I moved in the industry.

The sales ecosystem is huge! There are tons of areas within sales from which you can gain experience. These include being an individual contributor to working in leadership, training, analytics, sales technology, sales enablement, and much more. Many people start as an individual contributor and move into other areas of the industry, and some even become entrepreneurs, selling their services into the sales industry. The growth and career trajectory are endless. If you think about it, most industries and companies have a need for salespeople to market their company, and that is one job that I believe will never become obsolete.

What is one or more myths or negative perceptions about sales or women in sales that need dispelling?

There are so many myths and negative perceptions about the sales industry in general, but there are even more that specifically refer to women in sales. There could be a whole book dedicated to all the negativity in the world about women in sales. Here are a few that stand out to me:

1. Women with children cannot lead effectively.

Let's be real! Women are superheroes! We become pretty darn organized in setting schedules and deadlines dedicated to work and family time. Women know how to multi-task and can be fully present and simultaneously engaged caregivers for their family and very effective leaders. As a mother of three kids all within the ages of six to fourteen, I can tell you it is not always easy, but you push through any challenges that come your way. In 2020, when COVID-19 hit, I had three kids at home engaging in virtual learning—not to mention two puppies—along with my husband and me working virtually from home. I remember having to stick to a strict schedule morning, noon, and night, swapping between work and facilitating virtual school with the kids. My work still got done, I still had my prospecting calls and coaching calls for my reps and closed deals while maintaining the sanity of the household as it was new to all of us. My family became my "why" and my motivation to push harder. With strength, faith, and prayer, women can conquer anything!

2. Women of color are there to just check the diversity box.

I must admit it was not until the summer of 2020 when I really started getting concerned and taking action on diversity equity and inclusion efforts. I was completely naive to the fact that women like me were not given an equal and fair chance to move up the corporate ladder in sales. I thought I was moving up the ladder in a decent amount of time and was focused on just hitting my yearly goals in my compensation plan. I had a female boss who was a woman of color who motivated and helped me get to where I am, but most of my female colleagues had male bosses and were not given the same opportunities that I was given. After having a lot of great conversations with my husband about the Black Lives Matter movement and all that was going on in the world with police brutality against African Americans, I really started to understand the struggles of people of color in general but specifically women of color in sales. I read tons of articles about the absolutely low percentage of women in color not only in sales but the even lower percentages in sales leadership. It was truly an eye opener for me, and that is when I decided I have to amplify my voice as a woman of color and help to leave a better legacy for those who come behind me while trying to help pull the current ladies up on the same level with me. Women of color are innovative, creative, hardworking, ambitious, talented, resourceful, resilient, and communicative.

It has been stated and factual data given many times that hiring diverse talent makes companies better. According to People Management, diverse teams are 87% better at making decisions. I hear horror stories of women and especially women of color being told that they got the position on a board or in a company only because the board or company needed to be "more diverse." I call this crap! We have to ensure that we are hired because we belong there and that we are bringing our skills and talents to an organization that will make it better. Women in general are devalued in companies and this is taken into account even when you are a woman of color. The fact is that racial biases still exist, and we have to come to the realization that we all have to manage our biases, do our research, and take action to continue breaking down barriers. It is going to take a collective agreement and allies to make this better in the future.

What advice would you give to a young woman (or your 19-year-old self) who is considering a career in sales? What can anyone of any age do right now to prepare for a career in sales?

There are plenty of things that you can do to prepare for a career in sales. I would urge you to get into volunteer organizations that are meaningful to you. Volunteering goes a long way because it makes it natural and so easy to take on more responsibilities for an organization that's outside of your normal job description. This, in turn, helps you build more skillsets like multi-tasking and experiencing new adventures. When I was a young little girl, my mom put me in a popular youth organization for girls that is best known for its cookie sales. In it, I excelled, earning the highest achievement, the Gold Award. I remember kicking and screaming every year, thinking as I got older "I'm too big to be a scout!" Today, I am proud that my mom kept me in that organization because I gained so many skillsets that I still use today. From cookie selling, learning how to go out to prospects and talk about why they should buy these delicious cookies, and preparing presentations for the Gold Award, Girl Scouts taught me how to tell a story on paper, present it verbally, and build those communication skills in dealing with people in general. You will also gain customer service experience, which is a highly needed skill in sales. Thus, Girl Scouts was one of my new adventures that taught me lifelong skills that I use in sales today.

Build relationships and make connections whenever possible. This will help you to easily build rapport with total strangers because in sales, you meet a lot of new people whom you have to persuade and inform about the benefits and value to them in what you are selling. The saying of "be interested and be interesting" rings true in your relationships. You can cultivate relationships with people when you are interested in them as well as interesting to them.

Wisdom is gained as you experience life. Seek answers to your inquisitive questions as you travel along the way, especially when you do not understand. I say all the time to my colleagues and friends that you have to always be perfecting your craft and building your skillset, which just makes you a better person all around and can eventually make you more valuable to any industry you choose to make a career in. You will never grow staying in your comfort zone, so as you continue learning new skills, challenge yourself by getting out of your comfort zone, utilizing the skills, and trying new things.

Bring your whole self to what you sign up or volunteer for. If you volunteer to lead an effort or to be part of a committee, don't do the task partially. Bring your whole self to that task, give 150%, and be willing to learn from observation. Take constructive criticism, and understand that you will make some mistakes. Learn from them all, and do better. Trust me when I say people will see it, and it shows commitment.

Be your authentic self. According to a blog I read on the Imagine Health website, the definition of your authentic self is who you truly are as a person regardless of your occupation and regardless of the influence of others; it is an honest representation of you. To be authentic means not caring what others think about you. To be authentic is to be true to yourself through your thoughts, words, and actions. Be yourself, and don't cover up to make Corporate America feel good. That means wear your hair how you want, in a way that makes you feel confident, happy, and authentic. As an African American woman, I can identify with this. For years, I remember thinking about how I needed to wear my hair in Corporate America, avoiding wearing braids or my natural kinky curls so people would not think I was ghetto or that I didn't belong. I have been natural for many years, but instead of embracing my natural kinky and wavy curls, I would flat iron my hair straight all the time and always thought it would make me feel like I belonged. In 2020, after my oldest daughter, Shalon, decided to embrace her natural curls and start her natural hair journey, I started thinking about the idea. Shortly after, I followed in her footsteps and did the exact same thing. It felt like a relief in a sense because I got tons of compliments from colleagues, family, and friends about how great it looked. Now, do not get me wrong. I still like to change my style ever so often that now my colleagues never know what hairstyle I am going to have when I show up to a meeting; I feel great, and it is less time-consuming to do my hair. After all, the quote by an unknown author asserts "Self-confidence is the best outfit. Rock it, and own it." I could not agree with this more! It is not about how you look but about your values, skills, and talent that you bring to an organization.

Biography

Shawanda Roberts is a Vice President of Sales at Frost & Sullivan. In her current player and coach role, she is an individual contributor and leads a team of sales professionals who work with clients, helping them identify, prioritize, and implement their growth objectives through research and advisory services. She resides in San Antonio, Texas with her husband, Lonnie, and three beautiful children Shalon, Shannie, and Lonnie Jr. (Lj) who keep her busy.

Along with her work and family commitments, Shawanda also devotes her time, energy, and passion to outside organizations with a good mix of industry and community involvement where she has held several leadership positions. She is an active member of Alpha Kappa Alpha Sorority, Incorporated; Girl Scouts of America; New Dimensions Ministries; National Association of Women Sales Professionals; American Association of Inside Sales Professionals (AA-ISP); and GirlzWhoSell.

She is passionately known by others as a leader of connection and conviction and is one of San Antonio's Top 40 under 40 award honorees.

BE YOUR AUTHENTIC SELF

Caitlyn Gill
Director

What was your path to the sales industry?

We are all in sales. This is what I tell my students in the first class I teach every term at Oregon State. Some say some salespeople are born; others are made. For me, I was selling before I knew it was a career, and once I had a little taste, I knew there was no other career option for me.

My mom used to make wreaths that she sold at a local elementary school craft fair to earn money to buy Christmas presents. I loved making those wreaths with her—the smell of the apples drying in the oven and the hot glue burning my fingers as I helped glue them to the moss and intertwined branches of wood. What I loved more was being at the craft fairs at age seven and asking the people who would walk by our booth who they were shopping for, learning about the things that would make their holiday season special. And when we sold a wreath—oh boy!—the thrill of the sale was like riding my bike down a big hill with my arms thrown in the air.

My first real job was at a submarine sandwich shop. You may say, "That's not sales," but I would say every job has a sales aspect, even making sandwiches. Everything we do is sales, even at a sandwich shop. You can always add chips and a drink, extra cheese, extra meat. There is no commission in the process, but it was so much fun to engage with customers and make their experience special, especially if it meant I could draw their names in mustard on the bread.

There was a jewelry store across from the sandwich shop, and the jewelry salespeople would come in for lunch. I admired the men's and women's sharp clothes and always paid extra attention to make their lunch perfect. One day, the store owner asked if I would be interested in jewelry sales, and I, of course, said, "Yes!" I will never forget my interview; I had a bug that was going around, but there was no way I was going to miss my shot to have a job that would allow me to actually sell something. After the interview, I threw up outside of my car. But the interview went off without a hitch, and I got the job! I loved working at the jewelry store. From dressing up to go to work every day—no remote yoga pants videoconference set-up there!—to learning about each customer's upcoming engagement, apology, birthday, or just to say "I love you" present they were searching for. I learned through the art of discovery and how important listening is to the sales process. I broke monthly and annual in-store sales records and, within a short amount of time, was doing quite well for a sixteen-year-old high school student and had saved enough to buy my first car. I loved the freedom that unlimited commission potential gave and picked up extra shifts whenever possible. Upon leaving for college, I had saved enough to give me a nice financial pillow moving into my college career.

In college, I worked as a bartender (sales), waitress (sales), a hotel activities desk employee (sales), and even in my internship where I was writing press releases for the School of Communications, I was selling the college. I knew when I left the university, I wanted to pursue a sales career; I just needed a company to give me a shot. That shot came with a company called Sageworks. At Sageworks, I began my tech sales career selling a tool called Profitcents. In those days, we did not have the luxury of online professional networking; you were given a book with thousands of numbers and were told to start dialing. I made 150 calls a day every day to accountants and analysts. I was told "(insert the word) off" and was hung up on at least fifty times a day. They say that builds "character." I say it was part of the journey. I was just happy to click my heels to the elevator and to help the five to ten accountants that gave me the time of day. They say, in sales, you have to have grit, tough skin, and be able to handle rejection. I say all jobs come with parts we don't like. Being rejected is just a small part of a really amazing job.

The startup culture was perfect for me—a fast paced, easy acceleration from SDR to account executive to consultant and finally to a sales engineer, which may be the best sales job on earth. I was able to work with our clients to develop a new product and train the first 150 banks who used the product. The product was developed to help financial professionals make good credit decisions and was part of the product suite that took the company to acquisition. I moved on before that moment to Global Software where I spent the best twelve years of my career before moving to academia. At Global Software, I traveled the world, worked with thousands of clients as the Director of Sales Enablement, and helped the company through many acquisitions, resulting in it eventually becoming Insight Software.

Leaving Insight was incredibly hard, but the idea of teaching sales and the impact academic sales programs have on the future of young salespeople were too good to pass up. Today, I have the distinct privilege of leading the Oregon State Sales Academy as Director. I am proud to share that in the three years since starting the program, we have won multiple national titles at sales competitions as well as the Byron L. Newton Excellence in Undergraduate Teaching Award. I developed the program to influence the next generation of salespeople through industry connection, competition, and sales training. Our program is open to all Oregon State students, which means every year, we have hundreds of our students leaving their academic careers with sales training. Sales training was not offered when I was an undergrad, and I have the opportunity to teach the world's greatest profession to students. I pretty much have the best sales job on earth!

What motivated you to be in sales versus any other career?

I am a long-distance runner. This may seem like torture to many, but there is nothing more liberating than tying up your shoes and hitting a trail for hours on end, navigating through the forest and taking on obstacles as they come to ultimately see on foot the most beautiful and hidden parts of our great country.

Sales is a very similar sport. It is not for everyone. It takes self-discipline and training. It has high highs and low lows just like a marathon. It takes mental and physical stamina. The terrain/customers are diverse. The rewards are immense. As a salesperson, you have the privilege to help people every day. Just like a race, you have to work hard to get to the finish line with a client. It may take weeks, months, or even years to help a client. But once you get there, there is nothing sweeter than knowing because of your product or service, that client will be more efficient and effective.

Like long distance running, sales careers are dependent on your willingness to succeed. I was and still am a frustratingly independent person. In sales careers, your will work as a team, but your ultimate success is dependent on how hard you YOURSELF are willing to work. I loved this about the career.

When I left college, an innate understanding awoke in my soul that this was what I was supposed to do with my life. My mentality shifted into not if I would work in sales but how. As a mother of two beautiful daughters, my sales career allowed me to support my family and show my girls that women can earn just as much if not more than their male counterparts. I am incredibly grateful that I had that insight as my sales career has mentally and physically taken me to places that I never imagined, including my work in the non-governmental organization (NGO) sector.

I have sold in the tech industry for years, but my proudest sales experiences revolve around the work I do with NGOs. I have volunteered and fundraised for many organizations including Girls on the Run, The North Carolina Lunch Cancer Foundation, World Bicycle Relief, Corvallis Environmental Center and The Sub-Saharan Education Project (SSEP) where I serve as treasurer. Leaders of NGOs have to sell the idea of donating to their organization or cause, and having great salespeople on board can change truly change lives. I saw this in person when I ran a yoga retreat in Ghana for SSEP.

I am a certified yoga instructor and have taught in-studio as well as worked with the OSU men's basketball and football teams.

In 2019, I had the opportunity to lead a yoga retreat in Accra, Ghana for the Sub-Saharan Education Project (SSEP) where we took a group of professionals to Accra for ten days to explore our outreach projects as well as explore the wonders of Ghana while practicing yoga and meditation. Our mission at SSEP is to enrich the lives of women and children by increasing access to community-based educational opportunities. Over the course of ten days, I was able to see the impact of our work through the children who benefit from SSEP's scholarships and school builds. Sales can take many different shapes, and NGO sales can truly change lives.

At the end of the day, what I always tell my daughters is if you believe in what you do and work hard at it, you will be successful. Like running, you cannot get to the finish line without the belief that what you do matters and the desire to win.

What is one or more myths or negative perceptions about sales or women in sales that need dispelling?

A myth that needs dispelling is that men outperform their female counterparts, and women need to be aggressive to compete. A 2019 study by incentive solution provider Xactly reported that 86% of women achieved quota compared to 78% of men. We do not need to be aggressive to get there. We need to hone in on the strengths we all have inside of us.

Sales is about asking the right questions, building relationships, caring, and determining the best ways to solve problems. Sales is not about being aggressive, cheating to win, lying, or being greedy. Women naturally own the characteristics needed to be successful in sales. We are solution-oriented and excel at active listening, showing empathy, and building relationships. I am not saying men in sales do not have the ability to be empathetic and listen; I have many male colleagues who are wonderful listeners and who are empathetic. What I am saying is these are OUR natural talents as women, and we should be proud of what these strengths allow us to accomplish.

There have been many times in my career I've felt the need to perform, to put on a show, to act in a way that subtly manipulates the situation around me. It reminds me of all the times that I've felt powerless to say what I really think or do what I really believe for fear of being perceived as less than. What if we were to consistently tap into that deeply powerful part of ourselves that allows us to excel in the field of sales? What if we used our powers of empathy and presence to change the world around us? These traits are in all of us; they are our superpowers. They will allow us to continue to break glass ceilings and build new pathways for female success.

What advice would you give to a young woman (or your 19-year-old self) who is considering a career in sales? What can anyone of any age do right now to prepare for a career in sales?

Be your authentic self every step of the way. We all have our faults and our doubts but when you can approach your sales career from a place of honesty and authenticity, you will open more doors than if you try to fit into someone else's mold.

Being yourself can be scary. How do we know how clients or how our boss will respond to who we are rather than who we think they want us to be? We must be courageous enough to step into the world as we are and know that you may not be everyone's cup of tea.

Your clients will appreciate authenticity. Bringing your true self to every meeting will bring new ideas and thoughts to the board. There is nothing worse than the Google culture of perfectly curated responses and little to no unique thought or action.

Your team will appreciate your expression without expectation, judgment, or skirting around the truth. There is nothing better than a diverse team with a broad range of mindsets and backgrounds. This leads to more innovative thinking and ultimately more success for your customers.

Some of the best salespeople I know are ones who approach their clients authentically and with honesty every day. They take risks at the helm of the ship of insecurity. They live in the moment of the experience as it unfolds rather than masking behind a shadow of who they think they need to be.

As Oscar Wilde says, "Be yourself. Everyone else is taken."

Biography

Caitlyn Gill is the Director of the Oregon State Sales Academy and a Professor in the College of Business. In her dual role, Caitlyn utilizes her industry expertise to prepare the next generation of sales leaders at Oregon State University by providing sales education and industry-led workshops to students in all majors at Oregon State.

Caitlyn leads Oregon State's national championship winning sales team and was awarded the Byron L. Newton Excellence in Undergraduate Teaching Award in 2021.

Prior to joining OSU, Caitlyn spent twelve years at Insight Software as the Director of Solutions Engineering. Prior to Joining Insight, Caitlyn began her tech career with three years at Sageworks, now Abrigo, serving in sales, consulting, and management roles.

Caitlyn earned her MBA from the University of North Carolina at Chapel Hill where she served as a member of Women of MBA@ UNC, promoting the success of women in leadership. Caitlyn was also nominated by her class to serve as graduating class speaker.

Caitlyn serves on the executive board of the Sub-Saharan Education Project (SSEP) as treasurer and as well as a group travel leader. SSEP supports women and children's educational advancement in Ghana, cultivates partnerships with marginalized communities, invests in local resources, and helps to provide education to women and children living in extreme poverty.

Caitlyn is the proud mother of two amazing daughters, Sienna and Avonlea, and has one wonderful husband, Zach. In her spare time, you can find her and her family mountain biking, snowboarding, trail running, and hiking in the Pacific Northwest.

A LIFE OF SERVICE IS ONE YOU WILL NEVER REGRET

Lori Dunn
Director of Sales

What was your path to the sales industry?

The last thing I wanted was a sales career. From the outside looking in, I thought there was no way that this profession could touch the idea of the life I envisioned for myself. I had grand ideas of the kind of people around me and the mountains I could move with a lot of knowledge, love, and community. That woman was a connector. She knew lots of people in her communities that do unique things, so when a passing comment or a wish was made by someone, she knew exactly what introduction to make. She could help drive initiatives forward and make a real impact on those around her with the knowledge and understanding of her community. So, what was my dream? I wanted to be a teacher, leader, or negotiator—someone who helped empower and uplift communities with my training, heart, and the need to build a better world.

One day, I realized something in the world I was operating in wasn't working for me. When I combined the pace and structure of the organizations I worked in with the big vision I had for my future, something didn't add up. I wasn't on the right path. I wasn't making enough financially to do the things I wanted for this big life I had planned, and when I was alone with my thoughts, the goals and mission of my day-to-day tasks did not align either. So, I started attending events. I joined community after community, coffee chats, meetups, and mixers. The biggest takeaway was that no matter the profession, people can only tell me their small scope of the world—their lived experiences and ideas for what the career path they chose might do for them. And I didn't buy it. Their dream felt too far away from where they were, and by not being in those professions, I had no confidence in the outcome. So, I kept meeting people and gaining insight, trying to find my way forward. Then I met a sales leader; she looked me in the eye and said, "You should be in sales."

She got EVERY objection from me. "But I'm a connector, a leader, a negotiator, a teacher!" She explained that those are all the skills I would actively use and tap into in my sales career. I had allowed years to pass without exploring sales due to personal judgments I had about the profession, but talking to this sales leader changed all of that for me. Then I found my people. The sales pros who focus on helping their customers, who listen more than they speak, who learn the art and science of sales, and who don't do anything it takes to close a deal—they want real customers and to never force anything. So, I took a swan dive into the deep end of the pool and have never looked back. I even get to work for organizations that align with my values; it's what makes me excited to get out of bed and energized to meet with my customers. I work in clean energy and get to help decarbonize buildings and combat climate change every day—now as a sales leader.

What motivated you to be in sales versus any other career?

I'm not quite sure if I actively chose to be in sales. I was very focused on being a partnership builder—almost using that language to convince myself I wasn't a salesperson. Even though I knew I was in a sales role and everyone around me knew what my version of partnerships meant, I used it as a shield for a few months. Then I got stagnant; I wasn't seeing growth. I had to focus on getting training and support outside of my organization to grow; that meant being very honest that this was my first fulltime role in a tech sales role, and I needed help. The community stepped up to meet me. When that first role abruptly ended, I knew I had experienced my first #SalesFail, and it was time to own it, then take those learnings and find other growth opportunities.

Since I had been building a network of supporters who had watched me take the leap, own my mistakes, and be ready to dive in again, I wasn't alone. That's my favorite part about sales; you're rarely alone. My community helped me navigate finding a role in energy where the line to the social good is so prominent I had no objections, only excitement. Then the technical aspect of my sales role became a choice. I choose everyday to master both the science and craft of sales. I can be a great connector of people to new ideas and honor my social good life mission.

Now, I have a sales community and an energy community, and I get such joy by delighting my customers with the solutions I have for them. I'm a big researcher, and that has never failed me in sales. If you don't know why you are calling or emailing someone, then don't do it. So, I focus on research and having an honest discussion with my target audience. The research makes me feel prepared; the customers see that I care; and whether we work together or not, they just gained a fan, and I hope I did, too.

What is one or more myths or negative perceptions about sales or women in sales that need dispelling?

Sales is not slimy people doing anything they can to coerce people into spending their money. It's not preying on the weak nor is it a mind trap. Are there some salespeople who treat it that way? Sure, but I don't keep them in my community or refer them anywhere. Sales is full of curious people looking to have a business discussion to help make your day better.

Are there tactics and tools? Yes, but doesn't every job have those? In sales, you get to delve into human psychology, which is fascinating. I'm using different languages to paint a mental picture so my customers can envision their work with less of the annoying parts. I specifically focus on energy and sustainability. If that's what you do in your job and are bogged down by some outdated process, then I want to help you do it more efficiently. If I can help my customers get back to combating climate change, we all win. So, if changing the opening line in my email or asking a better follow-up question is a tactic, it's one I'm willing to use. A deal closed when the buyer isn't in control, loving the process, and getting excited by my solution is a bad deal. And sales is not about bad deals. If you come across a salesperson who makes your Spidey sense come alive, either ask them why or run.

It's pretty simple to sniff out the reason people do what they do. I've cultivated a community of people who want to do right by their customers. They span from energy, SaaS, B2B, B2C, and so many more. There is no common thread among us other than the desire to help people get rid of bad processes and get back to doing what they were meant to do. Can you imagine a world where everyone was siloed trying to combat climate change and living off a manual or, in the worst case, handwritten documents? If you didn't have a salesperson researching your company and trying to solve for a problem that you specifically have, that's where we'd be. I'd rather focus on becoming more efficient and building back the reputation of the profession. Let's flood the gates with salespeople who are here to make the world better.

What advice would you give to a young woman (or your 19-year-old self) who is considering a career in sales? What can anyone of any age do right now to prepare for a career in sales?

If I could talk to nineteen-year-old Lori, I'd tell her to stop over-thinking it. There are so many pivots your life takes; just try sales. But since little Lori is a planner—and frankly too ornery to hear those first few sentences—let's start here:

You don't know what is out there, so be open. Seek out mentors and advice from those who are a step ahead of you—not just in sales, but maybe you find you adore marketing or sales operations. There are many great next steps from your first foray into sales.

It's all about the people—start building your network today. Join online communities, go to conferences, talk to people in the industry. Make those conversations count.

Be very clear about what you want to learn, not how; don't try to control everything.

Do you care about what the company sells or simply that you can help people with your solution? Do you need a solution that hits a particular goal? (For me, it's a social good, hence, energy and climate change.) You can make a difference in many ways; the opportunities are endless.

Have a proclivity for action. I do. We can research for years, but the people who make a difference do something about their ideas and research. Don't claim you invented something when you didn't even try to produce it; that's looking backward. Realize you saw an opportunity and chose not to move forward, then do better next time.

Protect your peace. If that means you time block your days to get certain tasks done, do it. If that means you have a hard stop at the end of your day, do that. Each of us has our own rules that we've built around what we're willing to give a company. Stand strong because you can easily slip into eighty-hour weeks and wonder where your life went.

A life of service is one you will never regret. I repeat this often because it has never steered me wrong. In every aspect of my life, I have people who lift me up when I need it. That's because I've given so much to them until they don't blink at offering help to me. It's one of the great joys in life to have a strong community around you. Do this with your sales community; do this with your customers.

Biography

Lori is an advocate for social justice, DEI, sales, and bringing women into sales. She currently works as Director of Sales at InfiSense, which provides clean data to experts who are solving some of the world's toughest problems, combating climate change. She is President of the Board for Young Professionals in Energy (YPE) Boston and a mentor to many up-and-coming salespeople and programs to create more DEI in tech.

Before she entered sales, Lori spent her years in service as a Peace Corps Volunteer, building partnerships in nonprofits and government entities with the goal of connecting resources to the community members who could use them. Lori holds a bachelor's degree from California State University, Fullerton and a dual master's in Sustainability and Conflict from the Heller School at Brandeis University.

DON'T TAKE THE QUOTA AS YOUR TARGET

Shruti Kapoor
Founder-CEO

What was your path to the sales industry?

Let me start at the very beginning. I was born in Mainpuri—a small town in the hinterland of Uttar Pradesh (U.P.), India. The bias against women in U.P. is so high that female infanticide is prevalent, the gender ratio is skewed, and the government has banned sex determination during pregnancy.

Growing up as a girl was a mixed experience—my father was very progressive and focused on ensuring we got the best education and opportunities. However, a lot of the rest of the world looked at women with pity, as if we were damaged goods and liabilities on our families. As my way of over-compensating, I plunged myself into academics and was determined to make my place in the world by dazzling it with my intellect.

I got a full scholarship to study in Singapore when I was sixteen, an opportunity and a challenge that I embraced but not without fear. I studied life sciences, then decided to switch tracks to the business side of things with an MBA from India's most prestigious business school, Indian Institute of Management Ahmedabad (IIMA). I was always great with numbers, but when considering career choices, sales wasn't on my list. I started my career as an investment banker, then worked in finance for nearly a decade.

With ambitions of starting up, I joined a fin-tech startup. Here is when I got directly involved in the more traditional B2B sales. It was exhilarating, frustrating, and definitely required developing a thick skin to rejections. My path to sales was checkered, and I landed in sales much later in my career. I have a lot of catching up to do.

What motivated you to be in sales versus any other career?

All through the first decade of my career, sales was just under the surface. It was clear to me that sales made the world go 'round. The most successful bankers weren't the geeky folks who won because of complex analysis but because they were the best salespeople backed by a strong brand. During my time as an investment banker, I saw several great technologies languish since the inventor didn't know how to sell it. I also realized that sales wasn't just the traditional context of a company and a buyer. But sales really extended to a lot of other interactions, e.g., selling your idea at a meeting or to your spouse.

I had always been a reserved person, and sales wasn't a natural choice for me. It was out of my comfort zone of being analytical, intellectual, and quiet. However, I knew that sales wasn't a skill I could ignore even if I didn't want to be a professional salesperson forever.

I took up sales as a challenge and a learning opportunity. As I did more of it, I began to enjoy the human interactions, and selling became somewhat secondary. I could have continued to be an investment banker or an investor, but sales felt like the most important skill for any business. That made me step out of my comfort zone and embrace sales as a career.

During my career, I was also fortunate to work with many people who really enjoyed sales and who excelled at it. They made me shift my perception about sales as a sleazy profession to seeing it as a highly skilled one that truly helps the buyer. Observing this had the biggest impact in my career choice.

What is one or more myths or negative perceptions about sales or women in sales that need dispelling?

When I read *Lean In*, I was surprised to read how the same thing said by a man or woman could be perceived very differently. An assertive woman would get tagged bossy while the same thing said by a man would be labeled assertive.

A lot of buyers also carry that perception. Perhaps they get more easily offended by an assertive woman—making it harder for women as salespeople. This makes it harder for women to tread that fine line between being persistent and annoying.

Another myth is that women have an easier time in sales because of their looks and natural attraction to the opposite sex, given that a majority of buyers are male in most industries. I think this often works against women. They have to try harder to be taken seriously and not misunderstood when they are building rapport or keeping humor alive in interactions.

What advice would you give to a young woman (or your 19-year-old self) who is considering a career in sales? What can anyone of any age do right now to prepare for a career in sales?

Oh, I wish someone had given me this advice when I was younger:

1. Don't be shy to ask questions. I wouldn't ask my manager uncomfortable questions because I wanted to keep the peace. In hindsight, I should have asked much more—not to make it uncomfortable but so I could learn faster.
2. Be ambitious—don't take the quota as your target. Aim higher and be prepared to work out what you need to get there, e..g., what would I do to get two times my quota instead?
3. Promotions aren't served on platters—create them. Early in my career as an investment banker, I began to accept promotions as part of company-led processes, and that made sense given the size and structure of the organization. However, as I switched jobs, I continued to view the world through that lens.
4. If you don't like it, don't put up with it. Sexual harassment is unfortunately common. It can take many shapes and forms—colleagues, boss, peers at networking events, or your buyer. If there is something that doesn't feel right, immediately distance yourself from the situation. Sometimes it can be subtle—a sexual joke, an inappropriate description, or a look. But sometimes these things can be ways to test your boundaries in small increments until you don't know where things are crossing a line. It is best to get out of the situation before it gets to an uncomfortable place. Better safe than sorry! Here's a personal story: I was at a networking event in 2019. During a conversation with a

stranger, the person started using sexually charged language in the casual conversation around sales. I was surprised but also unprepared. The other folks in the group tried to change the topic, but the interventions didn't work. I excused myself to the restroom and switched to another group of people after that.

5. Compromise or miss out. As a woman with family commitments—kids, parents, or anything else—a late-night networking event might not work for you. If it is something your company is organizing, feel free to suggest other formats of networking events that are more inclusive. While these events are labeled "optional," they can have a disproportionate impact on your career trajectory. So don't miss them because they are inconvenient. Try to make them more convenient; other women will thank you, too.

Biography

Shruti is the founder and CEO of Wingman. Shruti loves *Iron Man*, and with Wingman she wants every sales team to have their own J.A.R.V.I.S! Shruti has worked across life sciences research, investment banking, technology investing, commercialization, product development, and fin-tech before plunging into entrepreneurship with Wingman.

Outside of work, Shruti enjoys podcasts and boardgames. Her five-year-old son is her Wingman in giving flight to many models of paper planes. If not for Wingman, Shruti would currently be a life coach.

START WITH A VERB

Toni Portmann
Possibilitarian, CEO, and Founder

What was your path to the sales industry?

My path to sales leadership began as a child—as a trail guide in the Rocky Mountains in Montana! Beginning at eight years of age, I began to lead the customers and sell the riders on the merits of the wild west. I found myself selling the features of the ride: flowers, mountains, cowboy lore, and horse fun facts. The more I listened to their questions and honed my delivery, the bigger tips I got! That was my first lesson in starting with a verb: Earn your tips!

I ran my own business at fourteen years of age, and when you run a business, you are always selling. As I ran my own string of horses, I learned how to manage objections around price and juggle the wants and needs of the customer. I learned to "match the horse to the rider" and differentiate horseback riding from the other vacation experiences. I realized we live in an experience economy as depicted in *The Experience Economy* by B. Joseph Pine II and James H. Gilmore, and as I worked to put myself through school, I graduated on a Friday and went to work for a multinational technology corporation on a Monday.

The most important sales call you ever make is your interview, and I interviewed with two large divisions within that technology corporation. One was technical, and one was administrative. One worked with computers, and one worked with people. I quickly learned my superpowers early: I like people, and I loved selling! As I learned to sell what a product or service can do for others, I found another verb: Serve the needs of the customer—whether it is your prospect, your internal customer, a hiring manager, or a colleague. Determine their problem, and help them solve it!

I also realized that people buy from people they like, and people don't care how much you know until they know how much you care! And once I realized that caring and serving worked, I beat all my quotas and quickly got promoted into management and leadership positions.

I was blessed to work for a big blue-chip company and was put on a fast track for high potential leaders in the years when companies invested in affirmative action programs and began to allow a woman to do a man's job. I found being a woman in sales was FUN! Most buyers were men, and all managers were men; so, the more I became a scholar of the art and skill of selling, I was better positioned to teach new hires how to sell! It was a tipping point when I realized that sales is a process, and selling is a skill! And I loved it! Learning is a verb!

Learning daily from the best and the brightest, I led sales and service organizations for the next four decades by starting with a verb—making sure that sales strategies were actionable and began with a verb, causing action, followed by the specific assignment of "who" (the responsible party or team) needed to do "what" (the action) by "when" (a defined timeframe). Make sure that the deadline is NLT ... no later than ... with no penalty for beating the date. Selling with purpose, process, and passion became my keys to success.

Being an "intrapreneur," a leader inside a company, and an entrepreneur, inventing, naming, branding, carving out, and growing six companies with 15,000 employees in sixteen countries and small founder-led companies in the US, my verbs included listening and learning from colleagues and leaders who had skills and talents that I didn't have, reading from the best-sellers and shamelessly stealing the ideas and best practices that worked for me, making mistakes, analyzing what I did that worked and what I did that didn't work, and embracing the advantages of being a resilient woman in a man's world.

My guiding verbs: Work hard; play hard!

What motivated you to be in sales versus any other career?

I was motivated to be in sales because I loved people; I loved winning; and I loved seeing a direct result of my actions resulting in compensation, promotion, lifetime relationships, and a sense of purpose and accomplishment. Selling is not work! It is a verb.

I found that to be good at sales, you didn't have to be the smartest or the prettiest, the most extroverted, or the life of the party—although I was!—but you do have to genuinely like people. You must like talking to them, listening to them, learning not only about their business but their lives and how your product or service could help them achieve their objectives or solve their problems. I was motivated and given energy through interacting with others. And I found that closing the sale was exhilarating! I loved getting the deal done, doing the job right, achieving the quota, exceeding the goal, being #1, leading the best branch office, creating the best division, and being recognized as an industry leader as a company. The rewards of money, title, recognition, and promotion were second to creating lifetime friends and colleagues who wanted to either have me on their team or wanted to be on my team! Achieving with others was rewarding and fulfilling.

When I had other jobs that were process, technological, or administrative in nature, I found myself always selling! Whether it was a new way to do something or a way to automate a process so the team could reach higher levels of creation and collaboration that included working with others to co-create, I found that every job requires sales. Selling ideas and persuading change, leading others, and teaching gave way to the realization that sales is in everything we do; we are always selling our services, thoughts, ideas, and perspectives to our associates, our bosses, the boards we serve on, and in our personal life—our friends, our families, and our communities. Simply put, selling made me happy. Influencing and motivating others to achieve more than they thought they could became a part of every job and every promotion. Sales was the path to purpose and contribution.

What is one or more myths or negative perceptions about sales or women in sales that need dispelling?

There may be negative perceptions about women in sales, but I do not think women should give them any power. A woman who commits to a career in sales has, in her very nature, the internal fortitude and drive that will dispel myths through performance and achievement, and she will earn the respect of her colleagues and peers regardless of gender.

A common perception of gender bias is that an aggressive man is a powerhouse, but an aggressive woman is a bitch. Nonsense! An assertive woman can appeal to both the feminine and masculine parts of every buyer, colleague, and community. The underlying nature of an assertive female nature creates trust and commands respect.

Another myth might be that women can't be in sales or sales management because they can't balance work and home. Quite the contrary. A key advantage to being a woman in sales is that a woman can maximize her earning potential and balance her life because she understands that her colleagues, employees, clients, and communities are an extension of her life. When a woman authentically contributes her part to the larger ecosystem of work-life balance, a woman appeals to the buyer in a way that extends beyond work. A woman in sales is seen as empathetic and caring. Women are trusted mothers, wives, sisters, and teachers, and women have a competitive advantage because the buyer or investor realizes that the woman will take care of them long after the deal is closed.

And the perspective that women are not born salespeople or leaders because they are not, by nature, risk-takers is simply not true. Women anticipate and mitigate risk! Pre-COVID-19, we worked to live, and now we live where we work. Women appreciate being dependent on others and the value of a team. A woman understands the value of being an individual contributor *and* an effective team player. Women know how critical it is to make sure she develops and communicates a shared understanding of expectations, wants, and needs. A strong woman knows and values both the individual and the collective team because the company or organization, much like a family, must commit to a lifetime of learning, building on differences, and working together toward a common goal. To paraphrase the American physician and automobile pioneer Horatio Nelson Jackson, women realize that you can't do today's job with yesterday's methods and be in business tomorrow; she understands the value of creating a culture of shared values where actions speak louder than words. A woman intuitively knows that working with others while appreciating and valuing differences in perspectives and cultures creates a richness in the daily pursuit of goals and a soft landing when things don't go exactly as planned. A woman uses her mental muscle and her empathy to navigate the ever-changing landscape of business and life.

Finally, women innately value diversity. Diversity simply delivers better outcomes! Learning and leveraging the contribution of those that were different from me became more important than conformity. Whether in a company of 15,000 employees or a company of fifteen employees, whether doing business in one country or in sixteen countries, it was critical that I embraced diversity of age, ethnicity, education levels, and skills regardless of race, ethnicity, sexual orientation, or religious perspectives. Respect for the individual and an appreciation for the unique contribution through diversity of ideas and experiences not only create a place where people want to work; that respect and appreciation produce superior outcomes. However, my male counterparts often felt more comfortable surrounding themselves with groupthink and those who looked and acted like them.

What advice would you give to a young woman (or your 19-year-old self) who is considering a career in sales? What can anyone of any age do right now to prepare for a career in sales?

My advice to a woman of any age who is considering a career in sales—because we can always change careers or direction—is to start with a verb! Starting with a verb will define action and deliver results! Here are some of my favorites:

Define your values: What is important to you? Jobs will change. Titles and compensation change. Companies and bosses change. Understand your "why" and make sure you focus on not only "what you are doing" but "why you are doing it." Remember your values are what will define what you do and how you will do it. Don't compromise on values—EVER.

Document your vision, mission, goals, and strategies—write them down! Whether it's a vision board, a journal, a diary, or a business plan, record them on an annual basis, if not more frequently. Develop and document your personal and professional goals, break them into bite-sized chunks—daily, weekly, monthly, quarterly, annually—then hold yourself accountable. Reflect, refine, and if something isn't working, start over; but make sure you document actionable steps to achieve your objectives.

Measure outcomes: What gets measured gets managed! Define SMART (specific, measurable, attainable, realistic, and time-specific) goals. Hold yourself and others accountable to the results. Care about outcomes, and make sure they are aligned with the mission and are contributing to the vision. Inspect what you expect and make sure you deliver results. Keep score!

Celebrate success: What gets rewarded gets repeated! Take time to recognize and reward the desired behavior. Take time to say "Thanks!" Give others credit, and celebrate YOUR successes. Every "yes" and successful sale and achievement of a goal or milestone needs to be acknowledged. You will inspire others and stay motivated if you appreciate and recognize your wins—big and small.

Be YOU: Be authentically you! You take yourself with you wherever you go, and as you apply your action verbs—respect, include, learn, listen, contribute, execute, motivate, inspire, measure, document, collaborate, invent and create—make sure you use your own unique style and approach coupled with your bias for action. Do things the way they work best for you. Observe the way the best and brightest say it or do it, then create your own personal brand and style with your own unique rhythm and flow.

Opt out: If you don't find your fit, if you are not aligned or having fun most of the time, if you find that you don't enjoy the work you do or the people with whom you work, self-select and opt out. It will be great for your soul, your heart, and your future, and the company will benefit. When values aren't aligned or you don't find your place within the team, do yourself and others a favor and say "thanks" and "goodbye." Life is too short.

Start with a verb: In one of my favorite books, *All I Ever Really Needed to Know I Learned in Kindergarten* by Robert Fulghum, I found these verbs to be the secret to success and to life.

"[S]hare everything; play fair; don't hit people; clean up your own mess; work some; think some; draw and paint some; sing and dance some; wonder some; play some; hold hands and stick together; watch out for traffic; look and listen ...," and here are my personal verbs of hope for you: every day, may you live, learn, love, and BE YOU!—unless you can be a unicorn, and then, always be a unicorn!

Biography

Toni Portmann is a serial entrepreneur who wants to inspire humanity through curiosity and imagination. With more than thirty-five years of leadership experience in board and executive management, Toni has spent her career in technology centric companies ranging from SaaS, PaaS, cyber, General Data Protection Regulation (GDPR), software and hardware, to support and services. Toni's corporate leadership includes building six companies as their chief executive officer with more than $600M in revenues and 15,000 employees in sixteen countries. Toni has held executive positions with Fortune 100 companies. Toni has served on public, private, and nonprofit boards including roles of chairman of the board as well as chair of nom/gov compensation and strategic planning committees. Toni loved her experience at IBM where she taught IBM Sales Training to new hires in sales! She especially loves being the board vice president of GirlzWhoSell! Toni loves skiing and hiking; her seven grandchildren; and her cat, Frank!

WORK SMART TO CONTROL YOUR DESTINY

Annie Roche (Mewborn)
Sales Manager

What was your path to the sales industry?

When I was ten years old, I thought I would be a doctor. As a child, I dreamed of being a pediatrician.

When I was around fifteen, I thought I would be a good lawyer...or a diplomat. In high school, I saw myself eventually working in the United Nations.

When I was twenty, I thought I should be an entrepreneur. In college, I was exposed to the world of "social entrepreneurship," and I was inspired by ideas and brands that make a lot of money and that make the world a better place at the same time. What could compete with that?

So, back to the question...why sales?

At twenty-one, I decided that diving into sales at an early-stage startup would give me the best education to run my own business one day.

In hindsight, I realize that sales scratches the itch for each professional aspiration I had growing up:

1. Sales allows me to uncover problems and prescribe solutions. In sales, I am able to help people solve problems like a doctor would do.
2. Sales allows me to challenge the status quo and negotiate. In sales, I am motivated to find win-win scenarios like a lawyer or diplomat would be.
3. Sales is the closest thing to starting your own business without all the risk. In sales, you run your own book of business like a CEO of your own sub-company.

The most successful startup founders are always their company's first salespeople.

How do you combine passions for diagnosing and solving issues, advocating and influencing positive change, and making a lot of money while doing it?

The answer to me is clear: SALES.

My preference being software sales.

What motivated you to be in sales versus any other career?

I was motivated to be in sales because I believed it was the best profession to hone my skills as an entrepreneur. I still do.

In addition to entrepreneurial motivation, I have always been money-motivated. In a sales career, I loved the principle that you could work hard—and smart—to ultimately control your own destiny in earning potential.

The Sales Development Representative (SDR) role in San Francisco, California that I took right out of college had a $100,000 on-target earnings (OTE) with uncapped commission.

Translated by my twenty-one-year-old self: "If I meet expectations, I'll make $100,000. If I exceed expectations, I can make much more." I'll be honest; the opportunity to make six figures right out of college was extremely appealing and another reason I decided on sales over any other career choice.

The scary part for my twenty-one-year-old self was the OTE was split 50/50, which is very common in tech. There was a $50,000 base salary and a $50,000 variable compensation if I hit the goals that were given to me.

The scarier part is San Francisco was the most expensive city in which to live in the entire country. A $50,000 salary wasn't going to cut it. In my mind, I had no option but to succeed.

The $100,000 OTE was very exciting. I couldn't pass up the opportunity, and I knew I had it in me to rise to the challenge.

What has kept me in sales? It's not all about the money.

It's the mental stimulation of my day-to-day work, the wonderful network I have built, the rapid career acceleration, and the earning power that's continued to grow year over year.

What is one or more myths or negative perceptions about sales or women in sales that need dispelling?

The biggest myth I've heard about sales is that great sellers are extroverts or that the best sellers have extroverted personalities.

I would not consider myself an extrovert, and I have been a top performer in every sales role throughout my career.

In a previous closing role, I was the #1 account executive out of ten in performance by revenue compared to my team of nine male counterparts.

Instead of giving too much attention to this myth, I'd like to redirect the conversation to ten reasons we need more women in tech sales:

1. Women achieve 8% higher quota attainment than men.
2. Women think differently.
3. Women are better listeners.
4. Women are better collaborators.
5. Women are more empathetic.
6. Women are just as capable as men when it comes to analyzing.
7. Women are just as capable as men when it comes to influencing.
8. We need more women role models for the next generation.
9. More women are taking on buying roles and are changing the customer base.
10. Diversity generates more revenue.

Yes, according to "The State of Gender Equality in Sales" report by Xactly, women achieve a higher quota attainment than men.

Listening, collaborating, and empathy are becoming increasingly important skills for high-tech sales professionals—all areas in which women tend to excel.

Other important skill sets for a successful sales professional include analyzing and influencing, and research indicates that women are just as capable in these areas as men.

I encourage readers to check out the following online articles to learn more:

- "Why Women Are the Future of B2B Sales" written by Andris A. Zoltners, PK Sinha, Sally E. Lorimer, Tania Lennon, and Emily Alexander and published on May 28, 2020 by *Harvard Business Review*.
- "Xactly Releases New Findings: 'The State of Gender Equality in Sales'" published on April 2, 2019.

What advice would you give to a young woman (or your 19-year-old self) who is considering a career in sales? What can anyone of any age do right now to prepare for a career in sales?

If you are a young woman considering a career in sales, I recommend you start by doing a strengths assessment.

Here are the top fifteen essential traits of highly successful salespeople, according to a 2020 Sales Hacker Block by Bhaswati Bhattacharyya:

1. Upbeat
2. Passionate
3. Creative
4. Empathetic
5. Accountable
6. Well-prepared
7. Tech-savvy
8. Highly engaged
9. Goal-oriented
10. Relationship driven
11. Hungry to succeed
12. Competitive
13. Multitasker
14. Curious
15. Good listener

If you believe you have twelve of these fifteen qualities, I'd tell you to go for it.

Check out the full article, "15 Essential Traits of Highly Successful Salespeople," written by Bhaswati Bhattacharyya and published online on December 28, 2020.

Once you've decided sales is the path for you, I encourage you to seek out at least two mentors. I recommend both a female and male mentor to offer you different perspectives.

Lastly, like most things in life, what you get out of a career in sales is directly related to the effort you put in. If you're going to go in, go all in. Sales is not for those looking for a 9-to-5.

This is probably controversial, but if you're looking for a 9-to-5, I'd consider other career paths.

The energy and time you invest early into your sales career will compound.

It's my belief that the inputs to a successful sales career are 50% effort and 50% skill. It takes time to build the skills for long term success, but what you may lack in skill early on, you can make up for in concentration of effort.

Biography

Annie Roche (Mewborn) started her sales career as a Sales Development Representative (SDR) then advanced into the roles of Senior SDR, Account Executive, Senior Account Executive, Sales Manager, then Mid-Market Sales Manager. She was a key contributor to a San Francisco-based software company's early-stage growth from $1 million to $10 million annual recurring revenue (ARR). (In October 2021, the company announced $30M Series B funding.) Currently, Annie is building out a world-class sales team and changing the way businesses communicate with consumers at a text message marketing firm that was listed #7 out of 50 on a professional networking site's 2021 Top Start Ups list.

ASK AND SOLVE

Brynne Tillman
CEO

What was your path to the sales industry?

I started my sales career in 1990, right out of college. As a bored inbound order-taker for a Fortune 1000 company, I began to ask my callers questions about their transactions and why they were purchasing specific products. I learned a lot about our clients' needs and how they used our solutions. I began to offer more appropriate products for their specific needs, which in many cases had a huge impact on their businesses.

By the time I was twenty-four, I was training an entire call center on how to evolve from order-takers to a sales solutions team.

I was soon promoted to the field when I fell in love with sales. I loved interacting with my prospects and clients, and I got great joy from helping them succeed. What I didn't love was the cold calling.

I recall sitting across from a client, staring at his overflowing Rolodex, thinking if I could get my hands on it for twenty minutes, I could identify who he knew that I wanted to meet, ask for introductions, and never have to make another cold call. But in 1992, it wasn't politically correct to say, "Mr. Client, may I thumb through your address book?"

Three decades later, that is what we have with a popular online professional networking site—the ability to search and filter our network's connections; identify who they know that we want a conversation with; and leverage our relationships for introductions, referrals, and permission to name-drop.

So, in 2013 I launched Social Sales Link, a company that helps sales professionals position themselves as thought leaders, attract buyers, and start more sales conversations. Through our corporate training programs, 12-Week LinkedIn Sales Accelerator for entrepreneurs and small teams, we have developed a powerful process that is easy to follow and that gets real results.

What motivated you to be in sales versus any other career?

I am an accidental salesperson. However, when I look back, I was always in sales. From my school days when I was a restaurant server, I recognized that if I enticed people to get appetizers and dessert, my tip went up. The key was to not just pitch a menu item but to ask them what they loved, then match what we had to offer to what they would most enjoy.

As I moved into the professional world, I kept doing that— asking and solving... asking and solving.

In every sales position I had, I was the one who the trainees sat with or drove with to learn the ropes. And, while I was a really good producer, I was an even better trainer.

My pathway took me in the sales training direction where I fell in love with helping other people succeed.

Today, I am running a LinkedIn sales training and coaching business, where I am hyper-focused on guiding sales professionals to prospect better by bringing value and insights and being a resource, inevitably leading to sales opportunities when the time is right.

What is one or more myths or negative perceptions about sales or women in sales that need dispelling?

Women rock at sales. We may do it differently, but we do it really well. And I never want to pigeonhole anyone or gender as I believe everyone is their own individual, so the following is a generalization (that I happen to fall under):

1. Women instinctively have empathy and compassion, which allows them to truly understand and even feel their prospect's challenges.
2. Women tend to be really good listeners and are naturally curious, allowing them to uncover the needs of their buyers, making it easier to solve their challenges.
3. Women have a strong emotional intelligence quotient, which leads to self-management, self-control, better leadership, and stronger cohesive working relationships.
4. Women can identify negative consequences of unmanaged emotions, allowing them to detach from taking it personally.
5. Women are nurturers and want to fix things that are broken, which is essential in truly helping your buyers, not just selling them your "stuff."

What advice would you give to a young woman (or your 19-year-old self) who is considering a career in sales? What can anyone of any age do right now to prepare for a career in sales?

For those looking to get into sales, make sure you pick the right path. Find something that you really love, that you believe in, that you can be highly successful at, and that will appropriately compensate you for your hard work.

I also recommend working with a more seasoned company that has a sales training program in place. In addition, make sure you have a supportive manager who has a coaching style. Sales can be hard to figure out by yourself, so the right support is key.

Next, become a sponge. Listen to sales podcasts, watch videos, and read or listen to sales books daily.

Shadow successful sales professionals in the company. They can lessen your learning curve and help you avoid mistakes that they made. However, be very careful not to pick up their bad habits.

Be curious. Ask to understand. Understand the challenges and the priorities your buyers have both personally and professionally.

Earn their business by showing up as a resource. Detach from what the prospect is worth to you, and attach to what you are worth to your prospect.

Lastly, journal what is working, what is not working, and what you'd like to start doing and check it weekly. Consider sharing it with your manager or mentor as her input can be very powerful. This will help your continuous improvement.

You are a problem-solver. You have the unique opportunity to impact your buyers' success. Be proud that you are a woman in sales.

Biography

Brynne Tillman is the LinkedIn Whisperer and CEO of Social Sales Link. For more than a decade, she has been teaching entrepreneurs, sales teams, and business leaders how to leverage LinkedIn for social selling.

As a former sales trainer and personal producer, Brynne adopted all the traditional sales techniques and adapted them to the new digital world. She guides professionals to establish a thought leader and subject matter expert brand, find and engage the right targeted market, and leverage clients and networking partners to turn warm introductions into qualified buyers.

In addition, Brynne is the co-host of the Making Sales Social podcast and author of *The LinkedIn Sales Playbook: A Tactical Guide to Social Selling.*

DEFY STEREOTYPES TO MAKE IT HAPPEN

Katherine McConnell
Startup Revenue Advisor

What was your path to the sales industry?

"How about a milkshake to go along with those fried clams?" I got my start hustling add-ons to happy hour revelers—I was fourteen and blessed enough to have a summer job at a beach hut on Fire Island, New York. When I got a smidge older, I was able to serve cocktails, and remembering customers' go-to drinks and upselling top-shelf liquor was the key to my success. I sold books door-to-door one college summer although that wasn't quite as much fun as the beach waitressing.

When the investment banks came to my college for on-campus recruiting, I planned to join my fellow economics majors on the mergers and acquisitions (M&A) path, but a recruiter recommended me for a debt and equity trading floor program. I saw this as a sign: In high school, I had persuaded my local rotary club to sponsor me to attend a Wall Street camp. I loved the energy and intensity of the trading floors, so this opportunity was very appealing to me.

Out of 5,000 applicants, only eight of us were hired, and I was the only woman. The hiring process gave me a small taste of what my life would become—one of perhaps forty women on a trading floor with more than 700 men, peak boom boom room, and years before #metoo. I offer these numbers not to humblebrag but to showcase the magnitude of the male-to-female ratios.

My program had us rotate through different groups to find a mutual match, so I had to be "on" and sell myself every day. Interacting with so many diverse departments and intense personalities all in high-pressure, high-risk situations was invaluable. I landed on the bond derivatives desk, working with the quantitative team to develop, market, and sell new products. It's a thrill for anyone to close $150 million deals with pricing that required advanced mathematics amidst live market movements, but I felt especially proud to be a woman, defying stereotypes to make it happen!

Over the years, while my career has encompassed roles beyond day-to-day sales, the key sales skills I learned in those early years—relationship building, collaborating, analyzing situations, problem-solving, adapting, and using metrics—have been incredibly beneficial. It's been a fun journey from the milkshakes. No matter where your career starts or where it takes you, the skills you can acquire from sales will have a positive impact on your opportunities and results.

What motivated you to be in sales versus any other career?

*My proudest moment in high school was being the first female to win the award for overall excellence in academics, athletics, leadership, and community service. The award had ALWAYS gone to male athletes—usually football players because the football booster club was the sponsor. Shattering that historical fact and norm fired me up to break more barriers.

Did I anticipate what it would really be like on a trading floor where only 3–5% of the staff were women? Well, not by a long shot, but I wasn't going to let the blatant sexism and seemingly covert touches of misogyny deter me. What mattered were the results, and I was determined to close deals to shatter more expectations and stereotypes.

What I love about sales is that there are clear metrics! Are they always perfect? No, but there is transparent precision in sales that can level the playing field versus other careers where the definition of success might be hazier, and my data nerd self loves that I can create measurable impacts.

Learning is one of my top three values, so the ability to fully use my endless curiosity, connect people and ideas, solve problems, and revel in the ever-evolving variety of sales hit my sweet spot. The premise that, for the most part, I have self-determination over my outcomes appeals to my need for freedom.

In general, there are oodles of reasons sales is a great career choice: income potential, access (more companies are doing away with requiring a college degree), and garnering skills that will always be in demand—problem-solving, creativity, relationship and consensus building, adaptability, conflict management, emotional intelligence, and resilience.

The cultural shift to embrace the viability of working-from-home has opened the floodgates on flexibility that, I hope, will allow more women and caregivers to know the wonders of a sales career.

*Fun fact: My sister won the award four years later!

What is one or more myths or negative perceptions about sales or women in sales that need dispelling?

We could spend pages and pages talking about negative perceptions in general—sales professionals are pushy, manipulative liars who care more about closing the deal and money than the customers ... oh, and they are always playing golf or dining in fine restaurants. The false, over-the-top depictions in the media perpetuate unfavorable, inaccurate stereotypes and create artificial barriers to entry for all.

But let's focus on the perception of women in sales—despite massive efforts to increase the visibility of women in sales and its viability as a great career choice, there is a sense that "sales is a man's job." There is a sense that we don't matter, that we won't fit in, that our perspectives will be ignored, that our voices will be unheard, that we don't have the skills, and that we inherently don't have the right constitution and innate character traits to be successful in sales. But NONE of that is true!!

The results are in. *Harvard Business Review*, which boldly proclaimed, "Women Are the Future of B2B Sales," and Gartner, Xactly, and Boston Consulting Group—just to name a few—have hard data that women are better at sales than men! Here are some stats from these studies:

- Women achieve 8% higher quota attainment than men.
- Women outperform men by 3% overall.
- Women-led teams have higher win and quota attainment rates at 94%, compared to teams led by men.
- Organizations with high levels of diversity outperform their counterparts, e.g., 15% more likely to have higher profits.

So, it's a win-win—companies can generate more revenue by pro-actively recruiting women and women can THRIVE. Yet, the unfounded narrative about women in sales has a disproportionately adverse impact on recruiting women to sales—this needs to change!!

The biggest myth I'd like to kibosh is that women are always tearing down other women. Ignoring the pervasive effect of the media pitting women against each other and the reality that any group will have a range of behaviors, it's been my experience that women are out there cheering for other women, lending a hand, giving a push, and focusing on the greater good of gender equity.

I honor the women who came before me, celebrate the women who stand beside me, and hope to inspire the women who come behind me.

What advice would you give to a young woman (or your 19-year-old self) who is considering a career in sales? What can anyone of any age do right now to prepare for a career in sales?

Women of all ages, please know you are not alone!

If you are thinking of entering the sales profession, it's never been more accessible! There are free online courses, certifications, sales training programs—some just for women—and a host of other resources to help you find your way.

If you are already in sales, even if you are "the only one" on your sales team, the women in sales tribe is ready to support you! There are tons of women in sales communities now—join one; join a bunch! These groups and communities offer a phenomenal way to connect with other women in sales, get and give advice, continue to learn, and develop as a professional and as a person. Become an ACTIVE member!

Everyone knows about mentors, and it doesn't have to be a big, complicated arrangement. Maybe it's just someone at your company or in your field. What are your goals? Who is currently where you want to be? Who seems to have respect and influence? What do you want out of the relationship, and what can you give? Like all other relationships, clarity and communication are key.

The idea of a personal board of directors has come to the forefront in recent years, and this is another great way to connect with people who will inspire, teach, and push you. At its core, this is a group of people who want to help you flourish personally and professionally. Different people can serve different needs—experts in your field, peers you trust, connectors, influencers, and someone who helps you optimize your overall wellness.

Three final thoughts—learn how to advocate for yourself, continue to develop your skills, and build up your online professional networking profile and activity!

Biography

Katherine McConnell connects people and ideas to create impact and revenue traction for early-stage startups. Starting as a teen, hustling add-on milkshakes at a beach hut, she landed on a Wall Street bond derivatives desk closing $150 million deals, then helped to launch New York's professional women's basketball team; served on the Board of USA Volleyball; and ran Burton Snowboard's global nonprofit youth development program, The Chill Foundation.

Katherine shifted gears from intrapreneurship to startups as a revenue strategy consultant; her recent work includes launching mentor-and-alumni networks for female founders and rural innovators to provide resources to underestimated founders.

Katherine has been included in Sales Hacker's Top Female Sales Practitioners For Your Next Panel, Presentation, or Podcast as well as Slintel's 35 Sales Experts You Need to Follow on LinkedIn and is a three-time LinkedIn Top 100 Sales Star. Katherine is a Williams College graduate and is passionate about increasing access, opportunity, and equity for women in sales.

ENTER FOR THE MONEY BUT STAY FOR THE RELATIONSHIPS

Sandy Zhen

Founder and Sales Recruiter

What was your path to the sales industry?

Since I was fourteen, my career goal was to be a psychologist. I attended college to pursue a Bachelor of Arts in Psychology. I was responsible for most of my college tuition because I had too much pride to depend on my parents. My relationship with them growing up was extremely volatile. The last thing I wanted was them holding over my head "I paid for your tuition." The college I chose required me to pay rent in another city along with the hefty tuition and textbooks. The reality was that I needed a job that paid above minimum wage if I didn't allow my parents to shoulder the financial burden. My ego and pride forced me to be resourceful and super scrappy to meet my financial obligations. Along the way, I became money-hungry. When push came to shove, I turned to sales as the solution.

During college, I took on credit card sales, retail banking, and retail telecommunication sales. I became a year-after-year president's club winner. I used creative ways to over-exceed my targets—cold calling and referrals. One day, while cold calling a customer to sell home phone and Internet, I was offered a referral to a business development representative role. The customer said, "You know you're a real hustler? You would be great at business development in software sales. Want a referral?" In 2018, I left retail telecommunication sales for my first sales job in Software-as-a-Service (SaaS).

I had every chance to pursue a master's degree in psychology, but I chose a sales career instead. I never regret abandoning my dreams to be a psychologist. I leaned into my gut and passion to take a leap of faith. SaaS stole my heart. I love the grind, hustle, and thrill that a sales career encompasses. I take so much pride in being the person who establishes, builds, and repairs the relationship between customers and all the companies I worked for. Being the reason why people buy is such a great honor to me. I entered sales for the money but stayed for the relationship-building and multi-dimensional impact that came with it. Falling into a sales career was an accident. My parttime job became my fulltime passion. I was a B2B SaaS seller for almost four years, recently founding my own recruiting and consulting company. From selling SaaS to finding great talent who sells SaaS, sales will always be forever a part of what I do.

What motivated you to be in sales versus any other career?

My reasons to be in sales definitely evolved over the growing years. I chose sales because commission is badass! It enabled me to be the cool college kid who paid off her tuition and ate well every day. Being in sales allowed me to exercise my competitive and creative side. I was addicted to the hustle, grit, and grind. I used sales to validate my ego and self-esteem as I grew up with very low confidence. Every sale I made was a confidence booster. Graduating from extrinsic motivation, I leaned on more intrinsic motivational factors to stay in sales. Being able to participate in a line of work that drives revenue from the ground up is an honorable contribution. I can proudly tell the world my role is the reason why the lights turn on in any company. I'm humbled to create so many meaningful relationships with prospects and clients.

As of 2021, my reasons to stay in sales are beyond monetary motives. I get to bring people together and help clients find solutions they wouldn't have otherwise found without my efforts. One sale translates to a new client relationship and a chance for the company to afford more resources and grow other functions. Sales is a magical and crucial business function. My contributions are always tangible and visible throughout the organization. It's this multi-faceted type of impact birthed from my relentless hustle that makes it so rewarding.

What is one or more myths or negative perceptions about sales or women in sales that need dispelling?

Very much like engineering and male-dominated careers, women are perceived not to be as aggressive, competitive, and competent. Sales is not about being aggressive, but rather it's about the ability to hedge on relationships and an excellent communication of value. Women are more thoughtful and better communicators and relationship-builders. What separates good salesmanship from mediocre salesmanship is the ability to nurture no-interest to buy-in over time through building rapport. Because I'm a woman, I encompass all these skills—even more than my male counterparts in sales. My relationship-building skills enable me to better generate referrals and repeat business and to offset not being as "aggressive" when compared to my male colleagues.

What advice would you give to a young woman (or your 19-year-old self) who is considering a career in sales? What can anyone of any age do right now to prepare for a career in sales?

1. Work on your self-worth and self-esteem before diving into a sales career. The ability to detach from the outcome and embrace rejection will allow robust resilience. When I first started in sales, every rejection took a huge hit on my ego. On the same note, every sale fed my ego with an all-time high. I let the bad days ruin my entire day, stifling my productivity. My emotions were so fluid, and I kept letting it dictate the flow of my day. It took me years to master a steady emotional state and to be resilient regardless of my results. It's important to remain level-headed to remain consistent with your motivation.

2. Work on fundamental skills that are often overlooked: active listening, creative copywriting, and well-articulated communication.

3. Have a self-competition mentality. To succeed in sales, you must avoid playing the comparison game with your peers. Sales is a job that naturally drives competition and one-upmanship among your colleagues. The minute you compare yourself to others' performance is another minute taken away from driving your own performance. Be your own competition and validation. True rock stars focus on being a better salesperson than they were yesterday.

Biography

Sandy Zhen is the proud founder of Recruiting & Coaching by Zhen. Prior to being an entrepreneur, she was a top performer in tech SaaS for four years. She was a passionate seller with a relentless hustle who used creative strategies to excel targets. While networking online as an Account Executive (AE), she helped many jobseekers. Sandy has been through job hunt struggles and wants to help others be better off. In ten months, she landed sixteen jobseekers into Sales Development Representative (SDR) and AE roles! Sandy began to capitalize on her impact by founding her recruiting and career coaching business. She is a sales talent recruiter and a career coach for jobseekers. She uses a wide range of coaching strategies and leverages connections in her broad network to get jobseekers hired. She is undeniably passionate about finding a home for every job seeker's passion. Sandy's mission is to advocate for candidates who have the right attitude, skills, and potential over experience to pivot into tech.

YOU DON'T HAVE TO DO IT ALONE

Vicki Gurney
Founder

What was your path to the sales industry?

I was a junior in high school when I got my first job in sales, and it included me asking, "Would you like fries with that?" I was upselling before I realized what upselling was! My first "real job" after college was with a Fortune 100 company in procurement then marketing. Often people say they fell into sales. I guess spending those first years in non-sales roles means that I made a conscious decision to be a sales professional!

Over the years, I've worked for companies ranging from Fortune 100 to startup (their first hire) and sold a variety of products and services: integrated circuit chips, boxer fans, ball bearings, dry cell batteries, computer keyboards, intimate apparel, residential real estate, used cars (for a short stint), and thermal binding systems before getting into tech sales. I spent the last decade selling independent technical testing on software source code and Software as a Service (SaaS) environments hosted by the top three cloud providers to clients ranging from Startups to Fortune 50 Companies. Doing all the things, alongside all the people, while experiencing the good and the bad as a woman in sales has made me the person I am today. I am on a mission to make the world of sales a better place overall, especially for the women coming up.

I took my desire to help others; the knowledge I've gained; and more importantly, the wisdom I've gathered over the years and started a sales consulting and coaching company. I get to help companies and individual contributors develop processes, build pipelines, and achieve financial goals daily. It's true when they say that if you are doing something you love, you will never work another day in your life.

What motivated you to be in sales versus any other career?

Two main motivators fueled my desire to choose a sales career. One is the ability to earn for my family, and the other is the ability to solve problems. I love problem-solving. Taking the pieces of a puzzle and figuring out the best solution for the desired outcome makes me happy.

My experience of juggling business travel and two elementary-aged children as a single parent for several years made me stronger and provided perspective for difficult times that followed. I look back at the travel; on-site client meetings; trade shows; business dinners; and even the headrush from sprinting through the airport in my suit, pantyhose, and three-inch heels with fondness and appreciation. I was blessed to experience so many new and exciting things. I attended many face-to-face meetings at companies ranging from solopreneur to Fortune 50 with people from a plethora of backgrounds, cultures, and personality types. Continually building relationships is a hallmark of a career in sales and one of my favorite parts of the job.

The stories I can tell from sales-related international travel alone would add two or three chapters to my story! Things like getting lost in Quebec in a snowstorm, not being able to read the road signs that were only in French, and driving around near panic for three hours before finding the highway. This was pre-GPS, back when we used a paper map to get around! Then there was the time I had dinner with a colleague in Antwerp in the coziest restaurant that only had six or seven tables. The entire place couldn't have been more than twelve feet wide. I was fortunate to dine at one of the two tables on the second level that overlooked the town center on a beautiful, snow flurried, winter night. The staircase to the second floor would not have passed the standard building code! It had very narrow and shallow steps, was crooked (not spiral), and there was no way to keep the diners on the first level from seeing up your dress because you had to hold on with both hands at all times. Then there was finding one of my favorite places on Earth—Bruges, Belgium, which is known for its lacemaking. Fun fact—my other favorite places are Paris, France, and Largs, Scotland.

What is one or more myths or negative perceptions about sales or women in sales that need dispelling?

Women in sales have always faced the challenge of working in predominately male groups under predominately male leadership. We didn't have allies, not even the other women on our teams.

A mindset of scarcity prevailed. So, it's no surprise that I spent my earlier years feeling like I was completely on my own. I managed to stay at the top of the leader board out of pure gumption and long hours.

I have great news for women in sales today. You don't have to do it alone! I witnessed quite a change in the world of sales in 2020 due to the pandemic. Everyone was forced to work from home and engage with technology in ways most of us hadn't before. We were introduced to online learning resources we didn't know existed. New online communities of like-minded people formed. Conversations continued with regularity. Questions were asked and answered. Relationships developed, and for the first time, I found myself in a community of sales professionals who are accessible, willing, and truly want to help each other. I can only imagine how much faster my early career would have grown if today's resources had been available.

I'd go as far as to say I found my tribe in late 2020 to early 2021 on a social audio app. I've forged strong relationships. I've been on the giving end and on the receiving end of coaching and account-ability. I've been the teacher and the student with the individuals in this group. We text and speak regularly, and we show up for each other—whatever that looks like at the time. I've never been the social media or networking type. I was able to find my place in this big world of sales, and you can, too!

What advice would you give to a young woman (or your 19-year-old self) who is considering a career in sales? What can anyone of any age do right now to prepare for a career in sales?

My advice is to prepare yourself by doing a lot of research! Listen to podcasts, attend live virtual events, and view recorded webinars on topics that are relevant to the industry and product or service you are considering. Find sales community groups that you identify with and attend their events. Some of these forums allow you to ask questions and get responses live. Others are focused on best practices and are hosted by subject matter experts. Pick three or four people and organizations that align with your values and are talking about the things you want to learn. Follow their social media and/or websites so you know what they are doing next and where you can find them. Take notice of others who are attending these events and who seem to have similar interests. It's a good idea to connect with these people on business-related social media platforms. It's a great way to build your personal support system and community.

Talk to women who work for the company you are considering. Talk to women who are in the same or a similar role within the industry. Do choose wisely when identifying the people, groups, and companies you trust. All of this will be well worth your effort as it will provide better alignment between your expectations and the reality of your choices.

Find the support you need and show up with curiosity and confidence. Two things I've always told my children—remember that no one is going to take care of you like you will (except your mom), and how can you expect someone else to believe in you if you don't believe in yourself?

Biography

Vicki Gurney is a sales consultant and coach. She has spent the last decade of her twenty-five plus years of sales experience in technology. Vicki draws from her curiosity and love for problem-solving to help companies and individual contributors develop processes, build pipeline, and achieve financial goals. She is passionate about helping others get to their next level. She works with sales leaders and individual contributors, primarily in tech startups.

Vicki is a champion for lifelong learning and growth. She is a trainer and a certified facilitator. She gives back to the sales community as a mentor through non-profit sales training organizations and moderates free sales forums three to four times a week. Her biggest joys come from helping others build confidence and excel in sales; crafting; DIY; and hanging out with Bella, her Golden Retriever.

YOU DETERMINE YOUR PATH

Jen Ferguson
Global Sales Onboarding Delivery Manager

What was your path to the sales industry?

I was in college when the company I was working for asked me if I'd like to travel the country and set up new stores. They moved me from New York to Florida where my career progressed. From retail to cigar clubs, my journey evolved. I became a general manager for a company with a retail store, jazz club, private members club, and more. My aha moment started with the conference rooms that I reserved for members.

While booking those conference rooms, I noticed the professional software salespeople. They came in with their prospects and met in the conference room. Before and after, they socialized, signing contracts with cigars and drinks.

What struck me was how much more time they spent before and after—the relationship-building. I knew I could do that. While I was working holidays and weekends, they were wrapping up their days early and building lasting connections.

I always had an interest in technology. I'd had an opportunity to work on websites, do inventory, and implement new technology.

I found a technology company and took a job as a secretary to get in the door. In my early thirties, I entered tech. I spent a couple of weeks as a secretary before becoming an account executive. I brought new technology to market, explored marketing, and built teams from the ground up. I learned sales operations and how to integrate systems and create scalable programs. I wrote playbooks and coached teams where I found my passion for training and learning.

Now, in my forties, I've earned my dream job at my dream company. During my journey, I got married, I became a mother of two children, and I made friendships that lasted the test of time. In my free time, I embrace every opportunity to empower other women to start their journeys.

My career in sales has given me fulfillment, and now I have the opportunity to help new technology salespeople be equipped for success. It's had its moments, but the triumphs and the learnings have been sweet.

What motivated you to be in sales versus any other career?

Why sales? I don't believe it was a conscious choice. I started working at sixteen in a retail store in upstate New York, and when I had the opportunity to travel, I took it. I always enjoyed meeting new people and presenting the value of the products I sold.

In retail, I learned about the value of the customer experience, that with a sense of urgency, you can create a great experience. Taking that into technology with me, I knew that is where I stood out from my peers. Those core values I learned early in my career became my differentiator.

In tech, my focus on the customer and my sense of urgency led me to be a top contributor. The sales profession is about being of service to others. Making friends and building relationships are happy bonuses.

Once you understand that being in sales means the focus is not about you, you are golden. It's about where you can make other people's lives better, where you add value.

What is one or more myths or negative perceptions about sales or women in sales that need dispelling?

A negative perception about sales is that salespeople are untrustworthy. The best salespeople invest in their customers' success—where they can help and bring value. Part of my mission is to change the face of sales that starts with the perception. That a person needs to be gregarious or a "closer" to be successful is not what matters. It is partnering with your customers to find the right solutions, being a trusted advisor, and delivering an excellent experience.

It is easy to visualize the *Wolf of Wall Street* when you think of salespeople. The reality is that anyone who saw Jordan Belfort's swagger in this day and age would run. Expectations of people have changed in general—not only in sales but in our society as a whole as empathy became a larger focus during our pandemic existence.

Sales is about listening to understand and seeking to help. It's partnering and building a relationship. It's making a positive impact today and beyond.

Doesn't that sound like fun?

It is. Along the way, there are trade shows, meetings, and events. There is meeting new people, learning, and growing. The one thing that is consistent in life is change; if you are adaptable and are ready for anything, then sales is for you. It's a lot of fun to change based on the needs of the customers, industry, and technology. It opens a world of opportunity.

What advice would you give to a young woman (or your 19-year-old self) who is considering a career in sales? What can anyone of any age do right now to prepare for a career in sales?

The advice I'd give to young women considering a career in sales is you don't know what you don't know. In every opportunity, there will be challenges and experiences. You will need to keep an open mind. Be willing to learn, grow, and not take anything for granted. Take in everything, but decide for yourself what to keep and what to let go. Be sure to explore what interests you and the opportunities presented. You determine your path. At the end of the day, the life you live is up to you.

Life is too short to suffer in silence if something is not serving you. Find the place where you feel seen, heard, and valued for what you bring to the table. Find mentors and a tribe—a personal board of directors to support you along the way.

There is so much opportunity in sales. The skills you learn and develop can take you in a number of directions when you determine what you are passionate about. With a beginner's mindset and a little curiosity, you will learn the skills to propel you forward.

The thing to remember is that any career is a journey. In sales, that journey can take you on new adventures as your skillsets adapt to changing trends to meet customer demands. Embrace every opportunity to learn something new.

Biography

Jen Ferguson is the global Sales Onboarding Delivery Manager for a popular customer relationship management service provider. She empowers and equips salespeople for success. She is recognized as one of LinkedIn's Top 100 Sales Stars with more than two decades of experience in sales, marketing, and leadership. As an award-winning sales leader, she has brought new solutions to market and built teams from the ground up. She brings value to the sales community as a mentor, speaker, and LinkedIn Live hostess. Jen believes in leading and selling with heart, that everyone should have the opportunity to be seen, heard, empowered, and valued at work.

THRIVE ON MAKING IT HAPPEN

Amelia Taylor
Account Executive

What was your path to the sales industry?

The cards you've been dealt, you must play. I am a firm believer in this statement, frankly, because we don't have any other choice.

In my thirty-one years of life, I have learned things the hard way, the easy way, the way less traveled, and by going against the crowd, but growth was and continues to be on my side, nonetheless.

For all of the cards I've had in my hand, I can say with certainty that I did not know how to play one single hand, but as the saying goes, "I decided to play the hell out of what I've been dealt."

That statement taught me a few big life lessons by doing exactly that.

Cards—favorable ones and unfavorable ones—have shown me and taught me that whatever page you're on in your own book of life with whatever cards in hand, you can't write down what will happen next; those lines are filled in. But as for the margins next to it, those are empty.

By the age of twenty-six, I found myself in a failing marriage. I had two little girls to care for and to put their futures ahead of the present circumstances I was facing.

The cards weren't pretty. I refused to let my lack of full clarity hinder my future to be a "pretty one" that my daughters would "thrive" from.

I chose to write in the margins of my book and to become the author by taking action with what little I had.

I chose to shift the "bad" hand I was dealt in that season of life to create the "good" that outweighs what the page read by filling in the blank margins even more so than what was already written...

I called this my "Marginal Privilege."

It gave me a sense of power beyond what I could control—that I had the privilege to choose what would go in the blank spaces next to my written pages and to shift my reactions as I read line by line, taking it one step at a time.

When push comes to shove, you do what you have to, especially when your children are looking at you, wondering what's next. By challenging myself on a daily basis, it was through those challenges where I insisted on remaining present and consistent in my pursuit of a life that I was fruitful, creating a solid foundation to stand on. It was then that I started to have clarity.

My girls—Rowan, age five, and Presley, age seven—and I now live in Tampa, Florida. Our family and friends are in Atlanta, Georgia where our roots run thick. Through the unforeseen circumstances life tossed our way, we found ourselves in a new place I'd later find was for the best. We found our home away from home—just us three—in a new city with new people, and survival mode was on high yet peace was fervently sought.

Valleys. Peaks. Challenge accepted. That was my mindset.

Because, simply put, life won't stop, so I can't stop learning to pivot when needed if I want to be the best I can be with tricky cards to play in one hand and two little girls in the other, trusting me to play with all I have with what I've got.

So, I did. I played. I quickly found a preschool I trusted for my girls and a cute house we called home through a real estate agent who learned my story and offered me a job working alongside him in Siesta Key, Florida. I was making it.

During this time, I learned a lot about myself that I had forgotten about myself. I learned again how independent I am, how I thrive off competition, how I challenge myself to be better than I was yesterday every single day. I lost my "grind and make it happen" mentality...and that was okay.

I started to see myself as the person I felt like I was supposed to be with the qualities that made Amelia...Amelia.

I knew I was good at sales. I knew I could talk to people. I knew I was smart enough to know nothing about something and still make something good come from it. I had the "it" qualities of a saleswoman.

In 2019 and 2020, I was working at a Software-as-a-Service (SaaS) company in St. Petersburg, Florida that I loved. Moreover, I loved the people I worked with. I knew, financially, it wasn't going to cut it, and the growth opportunities were limited—as a single mother trying to make ends meet, stability is key.

That's where I found the company I am with now that has allowed me to consciously and subconsciously grow in ways I never expected. I showed up, shared my goals and vision for what I wanted to achieve, and put my head down to work—I did just that, consciously. I created an enterprise division and became the liaison between sales and marketing. Subconsciously, I was learning account-based sales (ABS) and account-based marketing (ABM) approaches, business acumen, industry trends, and how to strategically plant seeds through developing long-term relationships with key players in the world of SaaS.

Sales is hard. But I am harder, and I am good at what I do. This I know to be true. There is so much to learn, and I say, "bring it on" to any challenge that comes my way.

I am proud of who I am, where I've been, who I've become, and who I strive to be daily as a driven individual, a loving mother, and a dedicated saleswoman.

The cards will continue to be dealt, but we get to choose what we put in the margins of our pages when playing our cards. Play on, and remember—life keeps going, so do you. Play the hell out of the cards you've been dealt.

What motivated you to be in sales versus any other career?

The more you put in, the more you get out. I know that if I consistently do the work—the daily hustle—and I take action and execute, I will plant seeds today that will turn into a fruitful garden down the road. If I don't take action, that's simply a choice of inaction. I never want to be someone who doesn't give their all to create what I can visualize my life being. Being in sales, I'm given the ability to choose my hand; to remain consistent; to build my brand; to make more than a base salary; to earn what I hustle for; and to have mentors who are dedicated to my growth and are in my corner, knowing what I am capable of. When your mindset is strong—and as we know to be true in sales—the battle is between your two ears. It's up to me, and it's up to you to remain positive and to make it happen, knowing the WHY behind the "making it happen."

Selling has always been a talent for me. Sales has been skill and talent combined. I fell into the SaaS sales world, and it absolutely has been and continues to be the greatest career choice that aligns with my goals and vision for myself and my daughters. Selling with a purpose—that's a winning strategy.

What is one or more myths or negative perceptions about sales or women in sales that need dispelling?

I once heard the saying, "Men are like waffles. Women are like spaghetti. Men can compartmentalize whereas women intertwine all aspects of life together."

I have always thought of myself as someone who compartmentalizes life—one "waffle square" at a time, if you will. I do believe women are more in touch with their emotional side, which I feel as though gives women a leg up in sales. We know how to leverage empathy and emotional intelligence on a deeper level. It's so important to let go of anything, everything, and everyone that brings negativity into your life. You are too good to be brought down, and you have to believe that. Take life as a challenge, remember your "why," and don't let anyone tell you what you can or can't do. You are the co-author of your own story, and that is a beautiful part of being a woman in sales! Make a difference, and stand out. It's in you.

What advice would you give to a young woman (or your 19-year-old self) who is considering a career in sales? What can anyone of any age do right now to prepare for a career in sales?

One of the most important things I've learned that I would absolutely share with a young woman considering a career in sales is that building your brand and finding the right support system within or outside of your organization is vital to your success. Work on you for you. Focus on what it is that you want to achieve, write it down, write it down as if it's already happened. Set the standard and set the goals for you. When you focus on yourself and ignore all those who don't believe in what you know you can make possible, you become a rebel who isn't afraid to color outside the lines. You build your brand by providing value-driven insights and having conversations with those who will root for you. Then, you will start becoming more and more confident through the momentum you've been building up. Momentum is the first step. If you see an opportunity, take it. Don't look around; look towards your goals set out for yourself. You can do ANYTHING you set your mind to!

Biography

Daily challenging the status quo by taking action with a strategic, yet rebellious mindset is who I am.

Through grit, learning my strengths, and knowing the value I provide, I put in the daily grind to create my hybrid role—Enterprise Sales and Strategic Growth.

Winning or learning, I am growing. Through growth, more opportunities will come, more wins, more losses; and ultimately, the knowledge of becoming the person I strive to be, professionally and personally, will present itself.

I am highly skilled in the art of unsolicited sales communication with the ability to capitalize on business acumen to drive and develop strong, long-term relationships with potential customers, clients, key influencers, and champions alike, understanding the importance of framing values per industry trend and persona.

I thrive on making it happen. I am a competitive, passionate, results-driven opportunist. I embrace change, and I adapt. I believe authenticity wins and am a fan of taking the risk as risks become one of two things: rewards or lessons.

REJECTION IS EVIDENT BUT QUITTING IS OPTIONAL

Natasha D'Souza
Program Manager

What was your path to the sales industry?

Surprisingly, my journey into sales that began in 2014 was by sheer accident. I was a freshman who had just graduated in media studies from a premier institute to pursue my passion in advertising. I found myself drawn to a start-up that was, at that time, quietly disrupting the food tech space in India, and they were looking for fresh blood to fuel expansion. I began as a sales manager, selling digital real estate, but within two months, I felt that sales wasn't my cup of tea. It challenged everything I really knew about myself until then—my confidence, my communication, my need to achieve. And when the process had completely dismantled my learnings about my personality, I had an epiphany. I was focusing on the outcome and not the input. So, I gave it all I had for another month, and in hindsight, it seems like I was reborn from the ashes—like a phoenix. I began enjoying reading people and conversing with them. I fell in love with solving problems and building trust. Trust is fact in the currency of sales with hard work being the capital.

I think it's fair to say I didn't choose sales; sales chose me. And thank goodness it did!

What motivated you to be in sales versus any other career?

Until 2019, sales wasn't the first career choice for Indian women. And since so few women made it into the industry, it was important to stand out. I was fortunate to be in the company of these pioneers—women who made success at sales look good, effortless even. They had a certain rhythm to the way they operated; it was nuanced and, at the same time, powerful. They weren't afraid to go above and beyond people's expectations. Their influence was pivotal in finding my anchor in sales. Along with this, I had the opportunity to discover a version of myself that taught me the art of improvisation; the value of listening; the gift of patience; and more importantly, the ability to deal with rejection. Once I had smaller wins, I began constructing bigger ones, and before I knew it, I had built a winning mindset. Subliminally, these made me take on tougher challenges and break the glass ceiling of my own personal achievement. It was like tasting blood; I wanted bigger and better wins. But they came with unforgiving lows. It took a few rather painful ones for me to realize that in sales, rejection is evident, but quitting is optional.

If you really think about it, the true craft of sales lies in making the same story more interesting every time you tell it.

To everyone who discouraged me from pursuing sales as a profession and told me "Don't consider sales," your sale failed.

What is one or more myths or negative perceptions about sales or women in sales that need dispelling?

People often do not treat sales as a profession; they treat it as a fallback career path in case their passions don't work out. Perceptively, it doesn't have the best pitch for itself as a career. There are targets to chase, numbers to crunch, and relationships to build and retain your business. This could mean long hours of networking and finding breakthroughs in an already male-dominated environment. But hang on! Don't mistake this for a woman not being able to be ridiculously good at it. In fact, here's where we lose most women applicants because they aren't able to see enough of us make it to the other side. But why not try? Like Wayne Gretsky says, "You miss 100% of the shots you don't take."

There are so many truth bombs waiting to be dropped. For instance, women need to travel a lot in a sales job. Let me tell you something interesting. It's been a liberating experience because in every new city, sales got me to discover, navigate, and explore the most optimum routes to reach from point A to point B. I've learnt the city's landscape, and it eventually became my compass to a new experience.

There is also an assumption that women aren't aggressive or persistent enough to have a stellar career in sales. But if the truth be told, we are engineered to perform well in tense situations and, therefore, are innately good at it. A stellar salesperson is great at time management and discipline. If you've ever wondered why bad products stick, it's because phenomenal salespeople do.

What advice would you give to a young woman (or your 19-year-old self) who is considering a career in sales? What can anyone of any age do right now to prepare for a career in sales?

Considering a career in sales requires a flexible mindset, especially if you are pivoting from an alternate line of business. Sales cycles tend to have various outcomes sometimes with a level of ambiguity that can get unsettling. But it could be a great foundational profession to pursue for the next step in your career. For instance, sales is an outcome of advertising and marketing, so exposure to the buyer's mindset could be an important initiation point. You also learn the art of building customer relationships and leveraging a business network—both of which are useful life skills. Your learning curve is transformational, especially since it is a male-dominated industry. You gain the virtue of standing apart—tall and confident. This profession has the power to unlock your potential through experimentation and improvisation as you interact with incredible people and get inspired by their stories. Trust the process of unravelling something new, something that is going to teach you a million ways to deal with "no." Don't let the numbers in sales intimidate you; instead, confront them. Let them become your steppingstones to victory. And the best part—you now instantly recognize when you're being sold to anywhere and at any time!

So, whenever you think it's overwhelming—something I have felt multiple times in my journey so far—I say quit tomorrow because if you truly fall in love with sales, then I hope tomorrow never comes.

Biography

I'm a firm believer that in sales, your personality is your best outfit, but ultimately, it's the numbers that do the talking. I endorse hard work and thrive on learning the psychology behind a sale. Through my pivot into people development, I look to invest in the leadership of the future. Recognizing, nurturing, and growing talent into the best versions of themselves—this is what drives me.

I like telling stories but love selling them. I'm on my way to building, shaping, and writing many more.

BECOME A BEACON
OF KNOWLEDGE

Jennifer Ives
*Global Digital Transformation
Executive*

What was your path to the sales industry?

My path to sales was the result of not putting blinders on throughout my career. Along the way, I have found that it is much more fun
to say "yes" to opportunities than to say "no," and saying "yes" led
to my first-ever sales job, which actually happened by accident.

About two years into a role as a geospatial engineer right out of
college and working at a fast-growing technology company, I was
asked to join our CEO for a meeting with our executive team and
a large client. The purpose was to discuss a project the client was

interested in pursuing; however, they were having challenges identifying the business outcome the project would achieve. Our CEO needed someone in the room with a technology background who also understood the importance of asking thoughtful questions to help uncover our client's true needs. I, of course, said "yes."

In essence, the "ask" was for me to suss out our client's pain and help craft an overarching solution—one that would drive value for our client. As it was originally described, there seemed to be a mismatch between our client's challenge and the solution we were in the process of crafting, and the business team believed it would be a good idea to bring in a technical team member to help.

Being a naturally curious and empathic person, I began asking questions and working to understand the pain our client's business was facing and the business outcome they were working to solve. We spent hours together, talking more deeply about their challenges, looking at alternatives, and keying in on the outcome they were working to achieve.

The meeting went so well that leadership asked me to continue to straddle the engineering and commercial teams to help with existing clients as well as meet with potential new clients and grow the business. This was my first step into a sales role, and I found myself thrilled by the thought of connecting solutions to solve pain points and, in turn, driving successful business outcomes.

To me, sales is just that—the process of identifying pain points and methodically crafting a solution for your client.

What motivated you to be in sales versus any other career?

At its core, sales is about problem solving. It is about removing obstacles and crafting workable solutions. It is the ability to quickly identify and understand the core of someone's pain, then tap into your empathy to craft a solution for that pain and drive success.

I often refer to this process as the "What medication is required?" question. For instance, does the pain the person or business is trying to solve require a painkiller or a gentle muscle relaxant? Once you have identified the type of pain, the solution is often quite apparent.

Sales is also about creativity, grit, and determination—it is an exciting career choice and one that will keep you on your toes and always learning. It is also a career with specific identifiers attached to success—numbers don't lie.

Sales and revenue generation roles allow you to become the go-to problem-solver. It is at the core of every business, and the fact that it is not a skill and a strategy taught in college or in business school is a missed opportunity. Without the ability to sell a product or a service and grow your client base, a business cannot drive revenue; it cannot make payroll, and it cannot keep the lights on.

Lastly, and most importantly, sales is a career that puts you at the center of the business. Sales leaders know their industry inside and out and often understand the market and see trends before others, becoming a beacon of knowledge and leadership within their organization.

What is one or more myths or negative perceptions about sales or women in sales that need dispelling?

The idea that sales is easy and that anyone can drive revenue is the number one myth we need to dispel. As they say, "If it were easy, everyone would be in sales."

Sales excellence requires curiosity and a love of learning that prompts you to constantly read, listen, and explore new ideas. Foundationally, an excellent sales professional is a relational and caring person, one who continually and consciously builds and maintains healthy connections with myriads of people and whose work flows out of this connection with others. To that, add dedication to improving skills in relating to clients and solving new problems. Also, determination to plow through all forms of obstacles and setbacks is essential. Finally, sales excellence requires the ability to create and drive a plan from initial thought through to closure. It requires taking control; claiming ownership of ideas; and, truthfully, becoming the CEO of your plan.

It also requires that you do what you say you are going to do. Commitment and follow-through are critical because your buyers depend on you to deliver. Clients are making, planning, implementing, and executing decisions based on your advice, often at the risk of their own reputation (and job security). This is the ideal career for someone who loves facing a challenge and succeeding.

What advice would you give to a young woman (or your 19-year-old self) who is considering a career in sales? What can anyone of any age do right now to prepare for a career in sales?

If you are reading this book, you are in sales or are considering a role in sales, so allow me to leave you with six thoughts on the topic because why stop at five? Five is so cliché.

1. Do it! Sales is one of the most exciting careers out there. It puts you in the driver's seat and helps guide a company's success. As a sales leader, you are at the tip of the spear when it comes to understanding the market, understanding where a product may or may not fit, and understanding pricing structures and what the market will—and will not—pay for services and/or a product.

2. Listen. A good ratio someone shared with me long ago was to listen 90% of the time and talk 10%. Become an expert and know your market—ask thoughtful, open-ended questions. Allow your clients to share fully with you—understand their needs and challenges. Learn from them and hone in on what

they need. By listening, you can better identify the type of pain they are in and, oftentimes, literally hear the solution.

3. Buckle up and lean into your problem-solving skills—your curiosity—and build your resiliency, two characteristics critical to a successful career in sales because you're going to be told "no" the majority of the time. Most things will not go your way—and that is okay—it is how you handle those moments that matter. Your resiliency will often come in handy.

4. Do not take things personally. You will face rejection often, which will very rarely be about you. It is generally about timing, internal politics, budgets, a committee of decision-makers you haven't yet uncovered, and many more reasons that you will need to identify and problem-solve to drive successful outcomes.

5. It is better to get to "no" early. A wonderful mentor taught me early in my career that it was better to identify if the answer was going to be a "no" as early as possible. Once you have identified this, provide guidance, and move forward versus spending time on a problem set that does not require your product or service. Be thoughtful, share advice, and keep in touch. Always grow your network because they just may need your product or services in the future.

6. Find a mentor early. Mentors can accelerate your knowledge and growth path. They can help guide you in honest and true ways— ways that are helpful specifically to you. A mentor might challenge you to take calculated risks and to try harder things while supporting you every step of the way, and their counsel can be essential at certain decision points between opportunities.

Biography

Jennifer Ives is an award-winning executive and product marketing strategy expert with more than twenty years of experience advising and leading global teams at the senior level, crafting revenue-generating business strategies, and driving double-digit growth results at technology and information services companies around the world. Her career reflects a demonstrated track record leading teams through technology and revenue-generating inflection points across numerous industries.

Jennifer was named to the prestigious Business Transformation 150 List and has been honored two times as a Top 50 Women in SaaS. She deeply believes in giving back to the business community and is an advisory board member for Institute for Excellence in Sales (IES): Women in Sales Leadership, a board member of Boolean Girl, a founding member of CHIEF, and a member of The Leadership Center for Excellence.

EARN THE RIGHT TO ASK FOR THE BUSINESS

Jenny Anderson-Frasier
Founder and Regional Director of Sales

What was your path to the sales industry?

Like you'll hear from many other women in this book, I didn't grow up thinking "I want to be a sales professional!" In fact, I didn't grow up saying I wanted to be much of anything.

You see, I grew up in generational poverty, spending most of my life on public assistance or hovering just above the cutoff for receiving help. The people I spent my childhood around were sailors, truck drivers, factory workers, and fast-food managers. Their "careers" were not by choice but because it was the best they could find and do. So, for me, a job or career felt more like an exercise of luck and survival than any intentional decision.

Looking back, if someone in my life would have known about sales as an actual career path, they probably would have recommended it. I was always asking questions, overcoming objections, and negotiating. Entrepreneurship even came easy to me. I can't tell you the number of times my parents got called because I was selling things on the playground—friendship bracelets, trading cards, braids in hair, even my own artwork. But I guess that's the problem for most women—no one tells us that sales is an actual career path, even when it's an obvious fit.

To be honest, I lucked into my first sales job. I was nineteen, a college dropout (okay, they kicked me out because my grades were so bad), had failed to make it as a flight attendant (long story short, 2004 flight crew wages were trash), and had just moved back in with my mom. In my semi-rural town and with minimal job experience, I turned to staffing agencies.

None would take me. I didn't have manufacturing or administrative experience. On my last stop, an agency recruiter suggested I go back to serving or apply for one of the few retail jobs in town. I went home crying because even the restaurants and retail jobs weren't calling me back. Then the recruiter called and said there was a local flooring store that was willing to talk to me.

The owner took the meeting only because he thought a former flight attendant would have great stories for him to listen to over lunch. I showed up more professional and well-spoken than anyone else and was offered the job. In a few months, my job went from answering phones and filling orders to handling advertising and doing trade shows. Coming home from my first trade show I told my mom "If I could just talk to people all day and make recommendations based on what they need, I'd just do that!" And for the first time in my life, someone told me "That's sales."

From then on, all my jobs were sales. For about ten years, I worked fulltime in retail, mostly in management roles. I enjoyed my job leading, training, and developing retail teams, and I was really great at taking new or underperforming locations and making them top-ranking teams. I hated the hours (forty-five plus a week), gave up a lot of nights and weekends (yuck!), and for less than great pay ($28,000 annually). So, when I had my second son, I knew something had to change.

I saw a job opening with a company a customer worked at, so I reached out to ask some questions. She was the hiring manager, said I'd be perfect, expedited the hiring process, and offered me my first B2B sales job.

I wasn't in the role very long before someone told me their bonus for the month—$7,000. That was three times what I made in a month in retail. It was like a switch flipped. For the first time in my life, financial stability was an option. Wealth was an option ... and I was the one in control!

I wasn't waiting for someone to walk into my building or call me first because I could prospect and create my own luck. If I followed the process, I'd find success. If I delivered on my promises, I'd get referrals. If I did these things consistently and with excellence, I could get promoted—and I was in just eight months!

That was just in 2016, and in that time, I've aggressively grown my career with very intentional job changes and choices. I've gone from an outside sales rep in rural Tennessee to managing a top 10% location for that company 2,000 miles away, transitioning to software sales as an individual contributor, taking over an entire inside sales organization for an Inc. 5000 company, and now leading a sales team at a tech unicorn.

Simply put, sales has changed my life.

What motivated you to be in sales versus any other career?

When I think about my sales career, I think about it in two phases— B2C/retail and B2B.

In retail, I was motivated by my ability to help and develop others and not needing a degree to do it. I was able to tap into my natural abilities—talking to people, curiosity, and leadership—to have a successful management career across multiple industries. Ultimately, that wasn't enough to keep me in sales, though.

When pregnant with my second son, I was actually planning to go back to school to become a midwife, but I couldn't get approved for student loans because I was in default status. (Judge all you want, but when you make poverty wages with a family of four and are on public assistance, student loans just aren't getting paid.)

Coming off maternity leave, I had three options—return to retail and struggle, stay home with the kids while my husband worked third shift an hour away, or find something else. (But what?!) I was really fortunate to have known someone who knew me, saw something in me that I didn't see in myself, and was a hiring manager for a B2B company.

That job and every job since has given me the opportunity to aggressively grow my career and income while also making an impact on the people with whom I work and businesses with which I partner.

In 2009, I was homeless. In 2016, I was a retail manager making just $28K a year, and all of that changed when I found my way to B2B sales in 2016. I've gone from living on food stamps and Women, Infants, and Children (WIC) government assistance to being in the top 2% of earners. Sales gave me a path out of poverty to prosperity. It changed my life. It changed the lives of my husband and children.

There aren't many jobs in this world that allow that kind of lifestyle change—certainly not in such little time and/or without a degree. My motivation in my professional and personal life is to continue to allow sales to change my life and the lives of others.

What is one or more myths or negative perceptions about sales or women in sales that need dispelling?

Myth 1: Women aren't good at sales.

My skin crawls when I hear someone say, "Women aren't good at sales."

It makes me especially angry if a woman is the one saying, "I'm not good at sales," and I call bullshit every time.

To me, it's like saying...

I'm not good at talking to people.
I'm not good at listening.
I'm not good at problem solving.
I'm not good at being nosy.
I'm not good at negotiating.
I'm not good at helping others.

Women spend our entire lives talking, communicating, and persuading. We're curious and nosy by nature. We ask lots of questions, we listen for what's being said, and dwell on what's not being said. We live for solving problems. What woman that you know hasn't offered advice when you went to her with a problem about a mutual friend, partner, or kid?

And negotiation and persuasion?! You can't show me a woman who didn't grow up bargaining with her parents to stay the night with so-and-so, have a later curfew, wear an article of clothing that her parents hated, or buy the newest electronic. Oh, and if you're a mom ... Well, sis, every day is practice in negotiation and persuasion with kids.

Women are made for sales.

Myth 2: Women don't work in sales because they don't like high pressure environments.

Again, I'm calling BS. But I won't spend too much time here because there's plenty of high-pressure professions where women make up the majority of the workforce.

- registered nurse (91% women)
- teaching (81%)
- social work (81%)
- counseling (79%)
- server (75%)
- human resource (69%)

Women don't avoid sales because of the pressure; they avoid sales environments that pressure people into buying/joining. (I'm looking at you, car sales and MLM!)

Sales should never be about pressuring someone into meeting or buying. Professional sales is a process of collaboration and consultation. You have to earn the right to ask for the business through trust and problem solving. Sales is what happens when you are fully immersed in serving your customer.

Myth 3: Sales is commission only.

I won't take much time here, but holy smokes, is that not true.

I've had only one sales job that was commission only. It was telemarketing—selling vacuums—and the only good that came out of that whole experience was I met my husband and didn't starve to death. (I did end up having a car repossessed and being homeless, though.) It was 2009, just after the economic crash, and was literally the only place hiring—please don't judge me!

But in B2B sales? I've always had a base salary ranging anywhere from $45,000 to $150,000 (up to $250,000 at quota) and haven't made less than $85,000 in any year since starting.

What advice would you give to a young woman (or your 19-year-old self) who is considering a career in sales? What can anyone of any age do right now to prepare for a career in sales?

There are so many resources out there until it can get overwhelming, but my best advice is to immerse yourself in the sales community.

There are so many places out there with FREE community, support, engagement, encouragement, training, and advocacy along your sales journey. By doing this, you'll learn the lingo, understand the landscape, build a network, get exposure to other opinions and skillsets, and (this is important) define and improve what value you bring.

Additionally, you can read sales books (this one is a good start!), listen to podcasts, watch YouTube videos, and attend webinars and training events.

Once you're ready to apply, you'll have a ton of social collateral and a good understanding of how to nail your job search.

If you want a little extra or one-on-one help, my inbox is always open to help!

Biography

I'm a B2B sales success story. I come from Appalachian roots and generational poverty, am the first woman in my family to not run moonshine or work in a shirt factory, and can say with pride "B2B sales changed my life." I've got a pretty crazy story of homelessness to six figures that I have no problem sharing and am a fierce advocate for women in sales as well as hiring people who CAN do the job over those who *have* done the job.

GREAT SELLERS FOLLOW A PROCESS

Liz Heiman
Founder and Chief Sales Strategist

What was your path to the sales industry?

Unlike many who accidentally venture into sales, I grew up in it. My father was one of the founders of Miller Heiman, Inc., the home of Strategic Selling™, and I was involved in the business for as long as I can remember.

My first job in the company was packing programs. Later, I conducted research and performed administrative work.

When I graduated from college, I created a marketing department, and eventually, I took on the Asia-Pacific division.

It was never my intention to go into the family business. I got my degrees in international political economy. I dreamed of working in the US Trade Representative's office. Then, 300 pages into my dissertation, I got frustrated and threw it in the trash. At about that time, I got a call from my parents who wanted me to run the Asia-Pacific division of the company, which at the time was losing money. It was a perfectly logical decision. They needed someone who knew their programs and philosophy and someone comfortable in Asia. I needed a job since I wasn't going to be a professor. They offered me double what a starting professor makes. I said "yes."

Up until that point, I had never been in a sales position. However, I had learned how to message when I was running marketing. I knew the basics of sales and the processes to follow to be successful. I was about to learn how to put into practice what I had learned. As the director of Asia Pacific, I was responsible for sales, marketing, training, event coordination, and managing a sales team. The kicker was that my sales team was five independent contractors who had been selling longer than I had been alive.

My very first sale was to them. I needed to earn credibility so they would not just work with me but would follow my lead. And I needed to convince them to start selling Conceptual Selling™ as well as Strategic Selling™. It took everything I had, but I did it.

My first customer sale was to the vice president of sales for a major carbonated soft drink manufacturer. I flew to Japan to meet him and see if I could improve our relationship and increase sales. When I walked in, his secretary said we had fifteen minutes. I panicked! Then, I calmed down, used my call plan, and got the answers I needed to improve the relationship. I walked out of his office forty-five minutes later with credibility, coaching time with his two elite teams, and a path to increasing sales to the manufacturer's Japan sales team. That was the moment I saw how the process and the passion fit together.

I implemented processes across the Asia-Pacific division, especially around the sales organization. I quickly learned that the most important of those processes was the funnel, which we lived and breathed. Once I had a functioning system, I mapped out our strategy and worked it every day, and as a result, we hit our numbers.

My passion for strategy and process grew over time. When I worked at Miller Heiman, I taught world-class enterprise sales organizations how to put structure into their sales. To this day, I hear from sellers how that process made them successful.

Working with smaller companies, I soon realized that their sales organizations had no structure or strategy. Instead, what they had was chaos, frustration, and disappointment. The cool thing is that I knew how to fix that. After helping countless companies, I developed programs to build sales operating systems that included the processes and strategies companies need to succeed. It is exciting to see the kind of impact it has on the success of an organization.

What motivated you to be in sales versus any other career?

I wasn't motivated to be a sales process consultant as much as I evolved into one. Having grown up in Miller Heiman, it was inevitable that I would develop sales skills. I read the books, listened to the tapes, and attended programs, so it was impossible not to learn and to, eventually, teach. What was surprising for me was how much I learned about process. Not only did the Miller Heiman programs teach process, but it was also process driven. We ran the sales processes we taught, and we had a process for everything we did in the company.

Having decided I was not going to have a career in sales, I went to graduate school to study international political economy. I studied things like economics, statistics, and methodology in addition to studying politics.

After grad school, I went to Miller Heiman to run Asia-Pacific until the company was sold when I went out on my own. It wasn't until I started consulting that I realized just how much that training would enhance my ability to develop process and strategy.

After I left Miller Heiman and started my own consulting company, I naturally gravitated toward sales and marketing. When process projects came across my desk, I took them as well. I was surprised how natural it was for me. What evolved from there was strategic planning consulting. At first, nonprofits asked for help, and soon it became part of my practice. It wasn't long before I discovered that I have a unique knack for building strategies focused on growth and sales.

My consulting company became increasingly focused on sales and marketing with an emphasis on building structure. I would go into a company, develop their strategic plan, then their marketing plan, then manage their sales and marketing effort.

Eventually, marketing became so complex and technical that I decided to focus on sales and sales processes. I have a combination of skills and experience that uniquely position me to create sales operating systems to help companies grow, and I love it.

I also love having control of my own income. I have my own business, I set my own prices, and I control my own sales efforts. I can balance my effort against my outcomes and make my own decisions about what is most effective for me.

What is one or more myths or negative perceptions about sales or women in sales that need dispelling?

Early in my career, I often heard men say, "Oh, she just got that because she is a woman." At first, it hurt my feelings. Then I realized that men who say things like that are looking for someone to blame for their failures. I had to realize that my success had nothing to do with their failures. There is no such thing as a "woman card."

You don't get to flash the "woman card" and get a free pass. If such a thing existed, women would comprise more than 20% of sales leaders. Women who get to the top get there on merit. No one handed them anything. More often, the hurdles were set higher because they *are* women. The "woman card" is a myth I would love to bust. When women are good at what they do, we need to reward them accordingly without caveat.

Another myth we need to dispel is that men are better sellers than women or that you need to be part of the "boys club" to succeed. That is utter nonsense. What is true is that sales is laced with the language of men. As a result, the traditional sales culture is aggressive and competitive. This "bro culture" has justified bad behavior by sellers by claiming "that's just how people in sales are." Bro culture has not been profitable for companies and has made it difficult for women to succeed in companies who reward this behavior. The data show that sales teams diverse in gender, culture, and race have better outcomes than teams without diversity.

The old archetype is wrong, and we need to open opportunities to a variety of people. Women who are good sellers need to have access to the same opportunities as men. But because women tend not to be as aggressive in their approach to sales, sales leaders don't give them high stakes deals. As a result, women often don't get to prove they can close those deals. We don't have to help women succeed in sales; we need to *let* them succeed.

What advice would you give to a young woman (or your 19-year-old self) who is considering a career in sales? What can anyone of any age do right now to prepare for a career in sales?

People think that sales is a job for extroverts with big personalities. That is old-fashioned thinking. Introverts and less gregarious people can be great sellers. Listening is just as important as talking when selling, and introverts tend to be better listeners. There are lots of options for sellers who are introverts. If you are curious, creative, and compassionate, you will be successful.

People often talk about sales as an art. The implication is that there is no process or order to it. Great artists will tell you that good art follows a process to get the right result. Great sellers follow a process. They are consistent and structured in their work. There is an art to communicating, listening, and solving problems, but that is only part of a sales rep's job. They also need to have a process to move leads through the funnel to close.

Sales is a great profession with the opportunity to make more money than most other professions. However, women avoid sales because they feel they can't afford to take the risk. There are many kinds of sales positions with different amounts of risk. Find a sales job that gives you the flexibility you need and that provides enough base salary to make you feel secure, then put together your plan, and blow your goals out of the water. It's a lot of work, but there is no reason to avoid it. If you like solving problems with people, you will like sales.

Many sales skills are essential business skills. For example, sellers need to ask questions, make presentations, and tell stories. They need to have meetings in-person, on the phone, or via video. Sellers need to use tools like calendars, scheduling programs, spreadsheets, and customer relationship management (CRM) programs. All of these are things you can start practicing right now.

Biography

Liz Heiman is the founder and structural thinker behind Regarding Sales LLC, a company focused on building B2B sales operating systems that drive extraordinary growth. Liz uses strategy and process to build a roadmap for success that focus her clients on getting the results they need.

Early in her career, Liz trained some of the world's powerhouse sales organizations. Using Strategic Selling™ and Conceptual Selling™ she helped them boost sales through enhancement of their sales processes and systems. Now her focus is start-up and mid-sized companies selling into complex environments including medical, government, and enterprise.

While most of Liz's customers build foundations that help them achieve sustainable year-over-year growth, others have realized exponential growth very quickly, one achieving $10 million in one year.

Liz is on a mission to challenge assumptions, build trust, and make founders' dreams come true.

TURN IMPOSSIBLE
INTO I'MPOSSIBLE

Meshell Baker
Authentic Selling Krusader

What was your path to the sales industry?

Finding a sales career has been one of my greatest joys—not my first choice or my original path, which was finance and accounting. I originally believed that attending college and majoring in a subject that would assure ease of employment would lead to a successful career and life. It wasn't long after landing my first job I discovered the disappointing daily grind of uninspired work.

The unexpected intervention of a career coach hired by my accounting team to facilitate teambuilding changed everything.

She offered me a complimentary career coaching session to assess my gifts and talents. The session included a review and discussion of the careers for which I would be best (better) suited. Her assessment tool of choice, the Myers-Briggs Type Indicator (MBTI), yielded results that highlighted career options of being either a lawyer, manager, or salesperson. I think you can guess what I chose—sales.

I wish I could report that my leap from accounting to sales was immediately successful, that I hit the ground running and easily ascended to the top of the leaderboard. No such luck. My initial sales role was selling Yellow Pages advertising space to businesses. I followed the script and found myself constantly frustrated, discouraged, and broke. If I'm honest, I updated my résumé and began looking to re-enter an accounting and finance career.

What changed? My manager changed. I went from being told what to do to being shown how to succeed. We established goals, milestones, and accountability to ensure my daily activities supported reaching my sales targets. I went from trying to sell to enjoying connecting with clients and prospects to share a valuable opportunity. What I took from that experience was the confidence to always interview my manager/employer about their initial and ongoing on-the-job training. With great tools and support, anyone can succeed in sales.

What motivated you to be in sales versus any other career?

As I have mentioned, sales was not how I envisioned my success. I thought I'd be an accountant at a large firm, crunching numbers and churning out spreadsheets. However, my destiny was met with an enlightened soul seeking to inspire others to live from the light within. I discovered that work with meaning could be fulfilling. Thus, I began my quest to experience more joy and enthusiasm in my day-to-day.

Autonomy and excitement were my top motivators for a sales career. I have truly loved being free(ish) in my day to day. The freedom of an autonomous job role requires accountability and responsibility to consistently deliver results. I've learned to focus my efforts on how I get to engage with so many amazingly unique and beautiful people on a daily basis. This awareness keeps me grateful and elevates my mindset and mood. It also makes the hard and challenging less daunting because its purpose is simply to support the amazing people.

Why do I write "free(ish)"? It's because working for a living is never 100% free. Whether you are an "interpreneur" in your current job role or an entrepreneur for yourself, success will always require learning and growing, which is uncomfortable and at times inconvenient. The adage "If it was easy, everyone would do it," still holds true for a reason. Success is work that is absolutely worth it.

The opportunity to venture into each day and meet new and amazing people brings joy to my heart. By seeking to improve my skills to ensure I am delivering memorable experiences and solutions has fueled my ease of selling, stellar reputation, and numerous accolades and awards. Knowing that I get to leave someone better off with more clarity for an informed decision is a powerfully motivating reason to keep selling.

What is one or more myths or negative perceptions about sales or women in sales that need dispelling?

You have to do it (sell) exactly the way you were taught. Following a script does not always assure sales success. There is so much room throughout the sales process to infuse your unique gifts and amazing personality. Did you know that 95% of our purchase decisions, according to Harvard Business School professor Gerald Zaltman, take place unconsciously? And it's people talking to people that make emotional connections, not features and benefits.

Being a minority woman in sales with a Rolodex of buyers and prospects who looked nothing like me, I found it impossible to mimic anyone else's selling style. It was my sense of overwhelm and frustration with trying to be someone I'm not that led me to seek support and guidance. During a women's mastermind, I discovered a powerful perspective shift. There is no one like me, there will never be another me, and no one can beat me at being me! This knowledge empowered me to wield my weird and beautiful personal style of selling. I have since built my brand on the principle of value first, money follows.

I encourage women in sales to be valuable. This is quite different from the "give to get" methodology whereas the latter often leads to overwhelm and resentment from give, give, and give more in hopes of getting a sale. Seeking to be valuable puts you in the driver's seat of your sales success. Establish a clear and compelling vision of what sales success means for you. Define who you want to be and why that's valuable to your big dreams, your ideal clients' problems, and your inspired connections goals. Cultivate valuable opportunities by understanding what motivates and inspires buyers, and nurture these relationships.

So often women find themselves selling in an uncomfortable environment, attempting to utilize unauthentic methods that only fuel feelings of fear, self-doubt, and imposter syndrome. Sales success requires consistent and ongoing conversations with strangers, hoping to establish familiarity. Without a confident belief in your value and worth, a sales career can quickly become an emotional and mental drain. Invest in creating and celebrating your unique and beautiful big picture vision of why and how you sell.

Remember everywhere you go, there you are. So become someone you are proud of and whom others are excited to meet. Build a daily and non-negotiable morning routine. Your success is dependent upon your relentless enthusiasm and resourceful curiosity. Life and business rarely go the way you plan or expect, yet it's always working in your favor. Your ability to quickly adapt to the unexpected, unpredictable, and unplanned with emotional maturity determines your ongoing sales success.

What advice would you give to a young woman (or your 19-year-old self) who is considering a career in sales? What can anyone of any age do right now to prepare for a career in sales?

Seek the wisdom of those who have successfully gone before you—find a mentor. No one succeeds alone, and everyone needs support and guidance to turn impossible into I'mPossible. Much of my early years in sales were hampered by my own insecurities, inexperience, the advice of the unsuccessful or a combination of the aforementioned. Oprah Winfrey says it best: "You don't become what you want. You become what you believe." Basically, your best investment is building your habit of believing in yourself.

The most powerful gift you can give yourself is establishing the standard and practice of confidence. Your success is rented, not owned, and the rent is due daily. Stay inspired and on fire for what lights you up and spark as many people as possible to experience joy and enthusiasm for their lives on your journey to success. Keep things as simple as your ABC's—Always Be Confident!

> "At the end of the day, we are accountable to ourselves—our success is a result of what we do."
> ~Catherine Pulsifer

Recognize that you are responsible for your life—the good and the bad—and be willing to change it. As a little girl, you fantasized about magic and miracles. You had no concept that mistakes would hinder or cripple your fantasies and fun. Find what fuels your passions, and put the pedal to the metal. Nothing amazing has ever been created without mistakes and repetition. So, get busy, and make some mistakes.

We all become but a memory in the end. And people always remember how someone made them feel. They especially recollect anyone who left them feeling loved and appreciated. You get to decide how you want to be remembered and if you will become the person who is recalled with fondness. The wonderful beauty of life is, at every moment of the day, you have endless opportunities to leave others better for having met you!

Biography

Meshell Baker is the owner of Meshell Baker Enterprises, founded to help business owners and sales leaders identify and convert more conversations with the ideal buyers they love working with. Meshell, along with her team, leverages her twenty-five plus years of sales and leadership success in more than a dozen countries to inspire energetic and collaborative communication that improves and increases business results.

Meshell is a Sales Confidence Igniter, an Authentic Selling Krusader, co-founder of Shift/Co Global Business Growth Community for Conscious Entrepreneurs, and an award-winning international keynote speaker. She is an amazing gift of clarity renowned for inspiring audiences to be less transactional and more experiential. She masterfully teaches her clients with her no-nonsense approach of transforming your obstacles into opportunities and your problems into profitability.

DISCOVER WHAT MAKES YOU EXCEPTIONAL

Wesleyne Greer

Sales Leadership Coach and Host of The Science of Selling STEM Podcast

What was your path to the sales industry?

When I started college, I decided to pursue a Bachelor of Science in Chemistry. Initially, I thought about being a medical doctor, but after a semester, I changed my mind although I knew I wanted to be some type of doctor one day. My end goal was to eventually get a PhD in chemistry. All my efforts were directed towards achieving that. That included doing summer internships and even an apprenticeship at a nuclear power plant. After graduating from college summa cum laude, I got a full assistantship to Rice University.

After just one semester, I told myself, "This is horrible. I don't want to do this for the next five years much less for the rest of my life." My next step was to use my degree, so I got a job as a chemist working in a lab. I was the person always asking questions like "Why am I doing this test?" "What's going on?" and "Who is this for?"

I spent five years as a polymer chemist, but I wasn't fulfilled. Before starting my journey out of the lab, I decided to cast a wide net for anything that I possibly could, using my degree. Fortunately, I got a job where they were looking for somebody who had a technical background but no sales experience. In those days, that was pretty much unheard. All companies wanted a ready-made salesperson.

Getting into sales through that job was the best career shift of my life. I finally figured out what I wanted to be when I grew up. I loved everything about sales and selling. Because of my love and my passion, I rose very quickly to the top of the leaderboards. In my first year selling, I hit my quota, and I was one of the top junior reps. Every single year as a salesperson, I met or exceeded my quota.

What motivated you to be in sales versus any other career?

As I was exploring the different things that I could do with my chemistry degree, I looked into supply chain, recruiting, and even thought about getting an advanced degree in engineering. There were so many different options available for somebody with a technical degree. I intentionally chose sales; I actually had three other non-sales job offers that I turned down. Sales presented me with the opportunity to have my own small business while a big company would be backing me.

For me, getting to go out and convince people to buy a product was so energizing because it perfectly matched my strong negotiation skills. My friends and family have always called me a "hustler" because of these winning negotiation skills. I loved that, in sales, I got to use my chemistry degree and my natural innate ability of hustling to convince people to buy from me.

What is one or more myths or negative perceptions about sales or women in sales that need dispelling?

There are so many myths around women in sales. One that stands out to me the most is that you can't have a family and be a saleswoman. So many times, people think the constant travel and working really long hours that come with a sales job means that it shouldn't be a career path for women, especially women of childbearing age.

I've had my fair share of experiences with that. I remember a job I interviewed for. It was one of those marathon interviews where they interview people all day and then take you to lunch. I recall saying something about spending time with my son, and I thought nothing of it. Once I got the job, I was told that having a son was one of the reservations management had about hiring me. They wondered how I would be able to travel all the time because I had kids.

I am living proof that a woman can have a family and be successful in sales. I actually had my youngest son when I was at the height of my sales career, exceeding my quota by doing double digits the year he was born.

My advice to any saleswoman with a family is always focus more on the quality of time that you spend with your kids and your family, not the quantity. A great example is spending two hours after school with them, doing something that they want to do, versus spending six hours with them watching TV and doing nothing meaningful.

What advice would you give to a young woman (or your 19-year-old self) who is considering a career in sales? What can anyone of any age do right now to prepare for a career in sales?

Sales is not dirty. It's not something you should turn your nose up at. I remember, in college, I used to think that business degrees were not hard to achieve—that anybody could achieve them. But later, I learned that business, sales, and marketing are rewarding, lucrative careers. Every woman has relevant skillsets to be good at sales, and they are innate. The characteristics that every woman has that make them excellent in their current career will make them good at sales.

So whatever people will tell you is annoying or that you should minimize is what's going to make you exceptional at sales. For me, that thing is asking questions. People used to always ask why I ask so many questions. Today, I earn a great living from my questioning ability. People pay me to teach them how to ask questions like I do.

Biography

As a former chemist that became an international sales manager, Wesleyne understands the challenge of being at the top of her game. Having managed multi-million-dollar teams, she marries her love for sales and her passion for coaching at Transformed Sales. Her management training improves sales leaders' capability of holding productive conversations with internal sales team members, which creates a collaborative, dynamic environment in which everyone feels supported.

With more than fifteen years in sales and leadership focused on the Science, Technology, Engineering and Manufacturing (STEM) fields, she empowers, coaches, and transforms managers into confident leaders. She understands that sales leadership requires both coaching to develop leadership skills and outside-the-box strategies to ensure everyone on the team becomes a sales superstar with a singular focus for her clients—more repeatable sales.

B2B IS HUMAN-TO-HUMAN

Anita Nielsen

Author, Beat the Bots: How Your Humanity Can Future-Proof Your Tech Sales Career

What was your path to the sales industry?

Like so many others, I stumbled into my sales career. When I completed my undergraduate degree in psychology, I wasn't sure what my graduate degree should be for. I had applied to a graduate school for journalism and was waiting for the decision when I took a temp job as an account manager at a small technology services company. It seemed like a good fit given I'd done exceptionally well working in several retail sales jobs. It never occurred to me that I could be in sales "when I grew up."

As an account manager, I fell in love with the work. I was interacting with individuals from all levels in organizations and helping solve their problems. My income was dependent upon my ability to connect with and influence people. I was *really* good at this, and the big dollars I was making were proof. It was so fulfilling and lucrative for me that when I got my acceptance letter into a prestigious journalism school, I found I didn't want to give up my job as an account manager to go back to school. Nope. I was going to stay at the job I was great at and loved so much. The rest, as they say, is history. Although I accidentally fell into a sales career, I could not be more grateful for that lucky accident.

What motivated you to be in sales versus any other career?

The more I interacted with my customers, the more they trusted me and wanted my help. I felt a great sense of pride knowing I'd solved challenges for clients and made a positive impact in their world. That pride is a powerful motivator. Similarly, it is incredibly gratifying when I ask existing clients for a referral, and they happily agree. Referrals are the result of a customer truly seeing the value in the work you've done for them. Inevitably, that motivates me to want to do more and be even better for clients.

What is one or more myths or negative perceptions about sales or women in sales that need dispelling?

Interestingly, I don't think there are dozens of negative perceptions about women in sales. There are a couple, though, that are so pervasive that they drown out the rest—good and bad. The perception about women sales professionals that I most frequently hear and loathe is that women are not strong or aggressive enough to be successful in sales. This is ridiculous and we need to put an end to it. In modern sales, aggression is <u>NOT</u> a strength. In fact, it typically ends up being a liability. Modern buyers want to be heard, not talked at, which is a hallmark of aggressive sales approaches. Women are socialized to be more empathetic and compassionate than men. Historically, women felt they had to take on the aggressive persona in order to win. This misguided belief results in women, tragically, hiding their natural tendency to be compassionate and empathetic so they can succeed in business. In modern sales, though, empathy is a powerful differentiator.

What advice would you give to a young woman (or your 19-year-old self) who is considering a career in sales? What can anyone of any age do right now to prepare for a career in sales?

I'd give anyone beginning a sales career, man or woman, the following advice: Choose to be compassionate, confident, sincere, and committed to creating success for your customers based on what success looks like for them. Be an advocate for their success, and your success will follow. Ultimately, in modern sales, who you are, what you stand for, and how you use that to create personalized value for your customers is the only true differentiator you have. Recognize that B2B is H2H (human-to-human), and in that human connection, you can make your magic. When you do it right, you will win bigger, better, and more while creating customers for life.

Biography

Anita Nielsen is the bestselling author of *Beat the Bots: How Your Humanity Can Future-Proof Your Tech Sales Career* and the President of LDK Advisory Services LLC.

As a sales enablement consultant and performance coach with more than twenty years of invaluable trench experience, she provides senior sales leaders with proven, custom sales training solutions based on the fundamentals of human psychology. Her training and coaching help level-up sales professionals and shape high performance sales cultures.

Additionally, Anita is committed to elevating women in sales and is a proud member of Women Sales Pros. She also serves on the advisory board for the National Association of Women Sales Professionals and the Women in Sales branch of the Institute for Excellence in Sales. Anita helps to educate, enable, and empower women sales professionals. She especially enjoys sharing her time and expertise with young women looking to succeed in their dream sales role.

DON'T SHY AWAY FROM THIS PROFESSION

Chantel George
CEO

What was your path to the sales industry?

I didn't know about sales as a career. Growing up as a first-generation American in a Caribbean community, I was unaware of what corporate sales meant or what it could be. The main voices in my head came from my father discussing what would be "stable" and "honorable" careers—becoming a lawyer or a doctor. Listening to his voice, after college, I applied to work as an advertising rep while I studied for the Law School Admission Test (LSAT). I recall walking into the office and interviewing by role play. It was not what I expected for my first corporate job, but something lit up inside me when I started objection handling with my hiring manager. Soon after I got the role as an associate account executive. I was in a sea of cold calling reps—approximately a hundred of us were hired at the time. All around me, I heard fellow reps getting hung up on, bells being rung when reps set appointments with business owners, and I saw large grins from reps who had good conversations.

I found out that our manager would send out midday call reports to help us stay motivated. I would look at my call volume compared to my colleagues'. I would get inspired to increase my output; I wanted to be the best. But I was one foot in and one foot out. In the back of my mind, I still saw myself as a lawyer.

Fast-forward several months later, I was one of the first to close a deal. I left the training environment and got put on a senior team. I was on the same team with the only other Black woman in the company. I was in awe at how she connected with business owners on the phone, and I was determined to emulate her. At this point, my friend started really hitting the gas on the lawyer track and started to be a little indifferent. She was taking practice LSAT classes, and I was having one-on-ones with my manager on the best sales books to read. I started practicing my pitch at night, and I showed up at work early to organize my desk. Most importantly, I started closing deals, and I loved the feeling of validation, recognition, and appreciation. No one cared that I was the new Black girl closing deals; my manager and my teammates just cared that I was contributing to their winning team. I was hooked.

Now, I have been a senior sales leader and mentor, and I run the largest global organization for women of color in sales—more than 4,000 members—called Sistas in Sales.

What motivated you to be in sales versus any other career?

Results. I am from a results-orientated family, and I am from a results-oriented community. I appreciated watching my manager write my deals on the white board, and I liked live experimenting with different objection handling and different openers. I felt like a scientist in a lab, working through different methodologies. I had a manager once replay my calls in a conference room and give me advice on my voice inflection, how I demonstrated value, and overall communication styles. At first, I was embarrassed, and I felt defensive. Then, I realized how adjusting minor things led to greater results. To this day, I am appreciative for all the sales leaders I have come across who have poured into me, who listened to me, and who spent extra time with me as I developed.

What is one or more myths or negative perceptions about sales or women in sales that need dispelling?

As I advanced in my career, most of the people I came across made comments that sales was a selfish career that is full of liars and deceitful people. Instead, I found earnest people, problem-solvers, motivated people. However, as a Black woman in sales, I came across prejudice, racism, and uncomfortable situations. While this may be very prevalent, it has not defined me. If you are in a minority, don't shy away from this profession. Despite the perception that sales may have or regardless of moving around the world as an "other," this is only one of the few careers that are merit based. Soon after, the deals start coming in, your confidence will grow, and you will be able to move mountains.

What advice would you give to a young woman (or your 19-year-old self) who is considering a career in sales? What can anyone of any age do right now to prepare for a career in sales?

I would tell my nineteen-year-old self to put one foot in front of the other always. Sales is a craft; it evolves and matures over time. There are thousands of methodologies, trainings, and sales styles out there. As you grow, you will find what works for you. Listen to your customers, and observe how they respond to you. At the end of the day, the core relationship is between you and them.

Biography

Chantel George is the founder of Sistas In Sales (SIS), the largest global organization for women of color in sales. She founded SIS out of a determination to promote, support, and encourage women of color in sales across all industries. SIS partners with Fortune 500 companies, tech start-ups, and consulting businesses to help them attract, hire, and retain women of color sales professionals. SIS also provides world-class training; networking opportunities; and above all else, a sisterhood for this underrepresented community.

Chantel is also an experienced Senior Enterprise Account Executive in AdTech, MarTech, and SaaS. With her attention to detail, thoroughness, and client-first mentality, she has exceeded quotas and trained and managed account executives as well as on-boarded larger scale clients for her previous companies.

Her work experience spans from public relations for an international cognac company to a four-year tenure as a senior account executive for the national business division of a company that publishes crowd-sourced reviews about businesses. She has worked as an Enterprise Account Executive enabling public relations for a New York-based company that specializes in artificial intelligence to provide real-time information to clients.

Chantel has worked with corporate communications professionals with the same technology that more than 400 newsrooms use to extract impactful events from a microblogging and social networking platform as well as for an online platform used for professional networking. She has served as a senior account executive for strategic tech B2B marketers and is currently a senior client partner.

PREPARE TO GO FROM ZERO TO SHERO

Janice B Gordon
The Customer Growth Expert

What was your path to the sales industry?

I sold from a young age. At age fifteen, I designed and tailored outfits and sold copies of my designs to anyone who asked. After completing my fashion textile and business degree, I was too impatient to create textile designs, and it was the business of selling that I loved. I sold textile designs in the USA and by the age of twenty-four, I represented an American company at European trade fairs. No one taught me to sell; I would research relevant people and call them. My English accent helped when I was in America and my European savvy when in Europe.

It was not until I was thirty that I gained formal sales training while working in financial services as an independent financial advisor selling to business owners and mid-cap companies. Here, my business experience helped me connect with founders and directors.

Without question, all the women I worked alongside were the most learned, accomplished relationship-builders and top achievers. On the other hand, my first sales manager left his wife and children for the younger office secretary (they are not together now); and when I met another of my sales directors twenty years later, he was an alcoholic, and his kids did not speak to him. This can be a brutal and rewarding industry; never lose yourself to the accolades and forget why you do what you do in the industry. Many of the women I worked with were single or single parents and wanted to give their children or their families a better life. They all had a grounding ambition, and this was their motivation that kept them focused.

What motivated you to be in sales versus any other career?

Unlike many others, I did not fall into sales. As an entrepreneur, I knew selling was an essential part of any business. I spent more than ten years in financial services from the mid-1990s. During this time, I built a profitable business. However, I fell out of love with all the politics. I loved the people and their stories, but the pain you had to go through to do an excellent job for your clients made the work untenable. By 2004, I had one too many experiences with bad sales managers. One sales director kept all the best leads for himself and was a passive-aggressive bully. Although human resources knew but because he was a company partner, they turned a blind eye to the director's bad behavior.

I was always motivated to help others, whether it landed in this quarter or the next. I loved the in-depth questions in the discovery process, then coaching the client through to the solution. Making the intangible tangible and getting client buy-in and commitment to an outcome is a significant skill in business across all industries and sectors.

You can see the relief when the buyer sees the outcome and the results they want; you helped them visualize and communicate it.

I felt remorse when the sales process ended as there was immediate management pressure to find another target. I always felt uncomfortable with the sales language—words like "killer," "hunter," and "target."

I understand much more about working in the right culture, choosing good managers, following your own path, or doing what feels right to you. I have built several businesses through nurturing relationships; all this I learnt from my experiences working in sales.

I am grateful that my sales training experience gave me the best business foundations that enabled me to start and grow several successful businesses. When I did my Executive MBA at Cranfield School of Management, one of the top UK business schools, I soon realized that this also gave me an advantage over some of my colleagues who may have achieved senior leadership positions in a functional area, but all they knew was that area of a business. When I was selling to a functional area, I needed to know the impact on the whole company whether operations, marketing, or finance. This gave me the agility to understand many moving parts of a business. I continue to leverage my sales skills in developing and coaching executives, founders, colleagues, and even family.

What is one or more myths or negative perceptions about sales or women in sales that need dispelling?

When I started working in formal sales, it was a macho culture: you hunt your target and kill! I did not identify with the hunter character that was the sales hero. Customers were targets, and it was all about the numbers. I felt like a failure in the sales industry because

I did not buy into this. However, with my client, I felt like a friendly guide helping them make a difference. I helped them be the hero or shero.

Having interviewed many women sales professionals who shared their experiences on the Scale Your Sales Podcast, I now realize that I was not alone in this feeling. They, too, did not buy into this fallacy but instead followed their savvy instincts of relationship-first. No one wants to be sold to, not even the hunter salesperson. No one wants to be treated like a piece of meat. The big myth in sales is that this is acceptable behavior. It is not! Buyers and customers will not put up with it anymore. If you do not treat people with the respect they deserve, you will not continue to be successful in this modern world. "Killer," "hunter," and "targets" are all terms and modes of selling that are outdated and do not work in this buyer-empowered world.

The myth is that women are less confident than men. I think women are more open and honest about the way they feel, and men hide or, because of societal norms, do not show their feelings. Studies suggest that the level of confidence women feel does not correlate with how confident they appear to others. In other words, women might feel really confident, but observers around them don't see it. The lesson, then, according to a 2018 *Harvard Business Review* article, is to stop telling women to feel more confident and to instead change organizational systems and processes so they treat men and women equally based on competence.

Another myth that annoys me is that women and diverse cultures need training programs and mentoring to help them cope with organization bias. I remember getting this one from a PhD research fellow during my MBA. Why are the minority groups the problem when it is the organization that perpetuates the bias and status quo? Organizations must adapt to the world around them if they want to be genuinely inclusive. Myth, the problem is yours. NO, the problem is theirs!

The big myth is that men are better at sales, while the statistics show that women are more successful in sales. Research shows that women salespeople often outperform men. A 2019 study by incentive solution provider Xactly reported that 86% of women achieved quota, compared to 78% of men. The B2B sales landscape has been shifting in ways that favor women in sales roles. And according to a 2020 *Harvard Business Review* article, it is believed the COVID-19 pandemic will lead to a step-change in this trend.

The industry must accept that the methods or language may be different between men and women, however, the impact and results are no less effective!

What advice would you give to a young woman (or your 19-year-old self) who is considering a career in sales? What can anyone of any age do right now to prepare for a career in sales?

Everything you learn in sales will make you better in business. Whether you use it as a starting point in your career or as a lifelong career, the skills you learn and the confidence you gain are the most transferable in business such that you will never regret your sales experience.

In managing your sales career, you can go from zero to hero very quickly. So always keep in mind that you are there to serve your clients and customers and that you represent a company to your own high standards, and if the company does not match your high standards of integrity, then find another company that does.

Take what you need to be the best you can be and leave the rest behind.

Early in your sales career, do your research, find great leaders and sales managers, and do not be afraid to move on quickly if you are not getting the support you need to do your best for your customers.

Your customers will remain loyal to you if you treat them with respect. This means you never waste their time, you do your research, and you actively listen and give them what they want and need rather than just what you sell.

Have a grounding ambition or motivating purpose of what you want to achieve and, most importantly, why, then stay true to your goal and personal integrity.

Sales is a fabulous profession, and even when you are working within a company or a sales team, you must be enterprising and business savvy. These skills you gain will quickly fuel your development—something you will not get in many other arenas.

Good luck, stay strong, trust your instincts, and have fun.

Biography

Janice B Gordon, The Customer Growth Expert, is the founder of Scale Your Sales Podcast and Framework. Scale Your Sales reimagines revenue growth through customer excellence and sales. With a distinguished entrepreneurial career as an international speaker, consultant, educator, and podcast host, Janice uses her thirty years of business, sales, customer experience, and leadership experience to unleash hidden potential and accelerate growth by investing in customer relationships. LinkedIn Sales recommends Janice B Gordon as a 15 Innovating Sales Influencers to Follow in 2021. She is also listed as a Top 50 Global Thought Leaders and Influencers on Customer Experience 2020 and 150 Women B2B Thought Leaders You Should Follow in 2021 and was awarded 25 on Sage Top 100 Global Business Influencer 2017.

Janice is a consultant, international speaker, trainer and facilitator, and author of *Business Evolution: Creating Growth in a Rapidly Changing World.*

STAND UP AND MAKE NOISE

Megan Killion
CEO and Founder

What was your path to the sales industry?

Let me take you back in time. It's 1995, and little girl Megan is writing her first ever play with her best friend, Becca. She writes, produces, and stars in her own show while selling tickets and concessions to the entire neighborhood. Megan takes home a WHOPPING $250 for the entire endeavor. She grows a bit older, and in 1998 Megan writes her first book of poetry simply titled *Moon Poems,* and after selling nearly 5,000 copies, Megan once again takes home a check. Yet, little ten-year-old Megan has still to hear the word "entrepreneur." In retrospect, adult Megan thinks that's quite a shame since it's clear to see this child is the definition of the word.

In 2002, Megan heads off to high school where she gets a stellar education from the international baccalaureate program at Sturgis Public Charter School. She coordinates multiple live performances, raises money for the school, starts clubs, becomes a political activist, works two jobs, and maintains "high honors." Still, no one is telling Megan about her leadership abilities or sales acumen. Megan gains early acceptance to all the colleges to which she had applied. She raises money to pay for college by creating and selling stickers with a group of other high school students. But then, Megan gets pregnant her senior year.

What a curveball.

I wasn't planning on getting pregnant in high school, and I don't think anyone who'd known me through childhood would've placed bets that I wouldn't be college-bound. I took a detour on my path to the top. I'm thankful that I did because had I gone to a private college, I likely would've accrued a great deal of debt, and I doubt I would have found my path to a career in sales and marketing, which I love.

Ultimately, I got my first taste of six-figure sales at my local community college re-selling college textbooks for less than the bookstore. I would get the bookstore price sheet for trade-ins, go knocking door-to-door in the dorms to buy books for just a little more than the bookstore would pay, then sell them online on a mega e-commerce site for a little less than the bookstore. I made six figures, but I caved to the pressure of the adults in my life telling me I needed to finish my degree and get a "real" job.

I ended up dropping out of community college during my third semester. I was trying to raise a baby, work two jobs, and juggle college. It wasn't working. Thankfully, fate dealt me a few more chances.

After the online retail book rush, I never totally put sales down. I worked at resorts, in hospitality, and in a couple retail jobs, but I always had a side hustle. I'd buy and sell on an e-commerce site or make small trinkets and sell them. Whatever. I knew I needed to make a better life for myself and my son. Without even knowing it, I was living the ABC life—"always be closing." Every conversation was about bettering myself and my career.

While working at a small local golf resort on Cape Cod, multiple customers offered me jobs working with them. I got an offer to move to Ireland and run an inn—not really an option as the single mother of a toddler but flattering and exciting, nonetheless. Another offer to come work at someone's financial firm left me feeling "out of sorts" as I never pictured myself in that type of role or lifestyle. At one point, a local came in and told me he'd heard of my excellent listening skills and ability to engage clientele. He offered me a role selling cell phones for one of the "giants," and that set my track in another direction altogether.

What motivated you to be in sales versus any other career?

At first, it was just about putting food on the table. At one point, I was a homeless single mom, baiting tackle for twenty dollars a bin. I was literally working my fingers to the bone in the freezing cold while my toddler slept in the back seat of my car. I got my bartending license to try and dig myself out of poverty. While serving drinks at a golf resort, multiple customers told me I'd be great at sales. I got a few job offers and took one with a cell phone reseller. Once I got a taste, I knew it was for me. The ability to control my income growth was incredible, and I learned I was extremely competitive. Seeing my name on the leaderboard each day flooded my brain with "the good chemicals." I've basically been a workaholic ever since.

Over time, my love of sales evolved. It isn't just about the rush of the hunt or winning. I genuinely love mapping solutions for my clients. It feels incredible to sit down with someone and have them tell you about all these problems that are causing them headaches, knowing you're going to turn things around from them. Admittedly, I have an ego. I love being the best at what I do, and I enjoy the level of respect that comes with this career when you're good at it.

What is one or more myths or negative perceptions about sales or women in sales that need dispelling?

I want every little girl who's told she's bossy to be told she has leadership skills. I am sick and tired of women being treated like we don't deserve a seat at the table. It drives me insane that many people don't recognize sales careers were built for and by men. The 24/7 work-a-holic salesperson is problematic. "Always available" isn't something to be proud of.

Women are seen as overly emotional, not aggressive enough, and a flight risk. The data say otherwise. A 2019 study by Xactly showed that 86% of women achieved quota, compared to 78% of men. Yet women make up less than a third of B2B sellers. Why is that? Well, maybe it's because job listings feature words like "ninja," "hustler," and "rock star." Or, perhaps, it's because B2B sales teams are often "all bros." If there's a keg in your office, stop asking yourself why you don't have more women applying for roles.

Gong, a revenue intelligence platform, recently released data stating that men had a 49% likelihood of moving opportunities to the next stage, while women boasted a 54% likelihood. They also showed that on average, women's win rates were 11% higher than men's. These data tell us, without a doubt, that the lack of women in the sales field is not due to a lack of sales acumen. Gong also stated in a March 2021 blog post entitled "Women are WAY Better than Men at this High-Value Sales Skill" by Devin Reed that women listen 16% more than men. Have you ever been asked in an interview what percentage of the time you listen to your prospects? No, me neither. But it's one of the top skills a salesperson can have.

Ultimately, the sales profession is outdated. There are harmful, outdated practices still circling to include passive aggressive sales tactics, instilling in young salespeople that they shouldn't take "no" for an answer. You *should* take "no" for an answer. You should respect people, and you should ask for permission to pitch. Sales is about value, respect, and rapport. It is about mapping solutions to pain points and painting a picture of a better future for your customer—none of which can be done if you don't first listen to them and their problems.

Despite the fact that women are better salespeople by the stats, men are more often promoted, especially into vice president and C-level roles.

Gender stereotypes kill confidence, and sales is full of them. Women are reluctant to share their ideas in groups, especially groups that are primarily made up of men. I am a confident, articulate woman, but when I was sitting on a leadership team made up of three White, heterosexual, cisgender men, I backed down on issues I knew I was right about all the time. None of these men knew more about sales or marketing than I, but I would let them win purely because I didn't want to argue. That's after a fifteen-year sales career with more than $500 million in pipeline influence. So, imagine if you're a young, fresh college grad.

Women churn out of sales roles faster for obvious reasons. Women are more often than not the primary caretakers of their children. Most of us are juggling kids, spouses, housework, and full-time jobs. Of course, we burn out, especially when we don't feel like we're listened to or valued. Women typically join the workforce later in life. Many take breaks to have children. So even simple things like having five plus years of experience in a job role can be casually sexist. If you want more women in your sales org, you need to start looking at work-life balance and your culture.

Ultimately, I believe women can have it all. Who says we can't? I have an incredible career, four kids, a loving relationship with my husband, a warm welcoming home, friends, pet projects, and charities I support. I've had to figure out a lot of things along the way and advocate for myself when maybe I shouldn't have had to. In my opinion, advocacy is the most important part. If I'm not willing to blaze a trail, then I can't really complain about the issues. We have to take action.

There's this common misconception that to be a good salesperson, you have to be aggressive and a hustler. I reject that. I don't push district managers to make bad decisions for the sake of my commission, and my network knows that. So, they buy from me, and they follow me from one job to another. I have clients now who I've been selling to for fifteen years—business owners who bought cell phones from me, then cloud systems, then security, content delivery networks (CDNs), and now marketing services. If you're good to people, they remember that. I've never hard-sold anyone in my life, and I've closed more than $100 million in sales.

I'm a people pleaser, and not everyone sees that as a good trait. But for me, being a people pleaser means I go above and beyond for my customers to make sure that they're getting what they need.

What advice would you give to a young woman (or your 19-year-old self) who is considering a career in sales? What can anyone of any age do right now to prepare for a career in sales?

- Like a popular athletic brand says, "just do it." I know not everyone is financially in a place to walk away from their day job, but start small.
- Networking is the key to professional growth. Talk to people who are where you want to be. Don't be afraid to ask "stupid questions."

- Invest in yourself. Take a class, buy a book, or get some one-on-one training to give yourself an edge.
- Stand up and make noise. Forge a way for the women behind you. Don't be afraid to lose your job over demanding you be treated decently.
- Don't let identity politics shape your destiny. You are who you are. That's a multi-dimensional person. Don't pigeonhole yourself to fit someone else's expectations.

Biography

Megan Killion has been in B2B technology sales and marketing for ten plus years with fifteen years of experience in general sales. She is a three-time founder and CEO of Megan Killion Consulting, Coven Cloud, and Vacation Hero. She loves a good book and unhealthy amounts of coffee. She's also a wife and mother of four boys.

DON'T GET MAD. GET CURIOUS.

Christina Brady
Chief Strategy Officer

What was your path to the sales industry?

I didn't dream of working in sales or even tech as a child. Really, though, who does? I find it fascinating how many incredible thought leaders and practitioners in this space find themselves stumbling into the realm of sales, SaaS, and tech. I'm no exception to that! As a lover of the arts and theater, I longed to be a performer and creator as a profession. Life threw me a curveball when both of my parents passed away within two years of each other when I was twenty. Effectively orphaned, my sisters and I found ourselves forced into the adult world far sooner than we expected. This also synced perfectly with one of the more devastating recessions in the near past, resulting in the loss of our childhood home. Insurance companies seemed to be the only industry hiring fresh-faced college grads, and when they tapped me, I jumped at the opportunity to earn more income than my current parttime retail job. After passing some initial testing and earning my licenses, I became a financial planner and dipped my toe in the pool of sales. I learned that I loved selling—the strategy; the problem solving; and most importantly, the ability to help others and improve their lives. The next step for me was obvious—find a product I love and go all in.

What motivated you to be in sales versus any other career?

I began my career in sales because at the time, it was seemingly the only option. It felt like less of a choice and more a matter of survival. I chose to stay in sales and dedicate my career to revenue teams and companies because I loved it. I still do! Sales isn't a one-size-fits-all. Over the course of my career, I've had the ability to impact the lives of my customers, leverage my creativity to solve complex problems, innovate on pitch and process, and learn the inner workings and drivers of some of the top tech products in the world. I've met incredible people and formed lifelong friendships. Working in sales as an individual contributor, leader, or executive is like nothing else in the world.

What is one or more myths or negative perceptions about sales or women in sales that need dispelling?

The largest myth that perpetuates is that women or anyone identifying as female is a "softer, more maternal" type of seller, suggesting perhaps that women aren't great in hunting roles at all and that, instead, should focus on supporting roles or relationship-building roles. If there is a top-performing female seller, she may be perceived as cold, unapproachable, or non-familial. This couldn't be further from the truth, which seems like an obvious thing to say, yet the myth is perpetuated. Your genetic make-up and/or chosen gender has no bearing whatsoever on your ability to succeed in sales (or, really, any other role, but we can talk about that later). Your passion, drive, skillset, learning mentality, and professional outlook determine your success.

What advice would you give to a young woman (or your 19-year-old self) who is considering a career in sales? What can anyone of any age do right now to prepare for a career in sales?

My biggest piece of advice is don't get mad; get curious. This industry and these roles can be life-changing but simultaneously difficult mentally and emotionally. Remember, when times are hard, you aren't being buried, you're being planted. Every hardship is an opportunity for growth, so aim to make the difficult days worth something! Also, aim high—you have no ceiling, and you are enough. You are more than enough, and if working in sales is your passion, the industry is better with you in it.

Biography

With fifteen plus years of overall sales experience and ten plus in leadership for B2B tech companies, Christina has a proven track record of leading organizations to growth and profitability through creative, strategic, and targeted global and domestic sales. She has a genuine passion for building culture, coaching, developing leaders, and producing top-performing sales teams across small to enterprise organizations in various industries. Christina uses her experience to impact and support B2B tech organizations across the US in her role on the executive team at Sales Assembly where she is also building out new programs and participating in ongoing public speaking engagements. On a daily basis, she is energized by the opportunity to help companies of all sizes scale at scale.

FIND NEW HOPES AND DREAMS AND FORGE A NEW PATH

Ginnette Baker
Vice President, Business Development

What was your path to the sales industry?

I remember sitting in my high school assistant principal's office and the look on his face—one of disgust and disappointment. The truth was out. I was pregnant. And with graduation just a few months away, he looked at me and said, "You just threw it all away. You ruined your life." I was stunned, mortified, and seriously terrified. I was editor of the school newspaper, a student council member, and former cheerleading captain all while volunteering at my church and working two jobs. I was already accepted into a top university with one of the best journalism programs to which I had won an editorial scholarship award that previous summer. I was well on the path of my dream to "get out" of the small town and make a difference in the world. In a blink of an eye, everything I had strived for was gone, and the man sitting across from me made me feel a moment of helplessness. What was I going to do now?

I had two options at that point; I could listen to the disappointed assistant principal and so many others and resolve that I had indeed given up all my hopes and dreams, or I could find new ones and forge a new path. In my heart, I knew God had a new path for me, and although I might not have made the best choices in the past, I knew that even with the tough road ahead, I wasn't alone as long as I had faith. My seventeen-year-old self would have never imagined my career path let alone that I would end up as a successful woman in sales.

Shortly after finding out I was pregnant and then graduating, I got a job at a small local credit union. I spent four years there, learning everything I could. If there was a chance to learn something new, I volunteered! If they needed help with loans, marketing, supervising tellers, or planning community involvement activities, I raised my hand. However, even though I was raising my son and was a young wife, new mom, and working fulltime, I still wanted more! So, I enrolled into a local community college and started working towards my college degree. While at school, I decided I needed to change jobs and find a larger company to grow as a leader and to grow financially.

I was warned that changing jobs would be a bad idea, that a large company wouldn't give me the flexibility that I needed to go to school and to be a mom. But I had faith. I knew it was the right path even though I actually took a tiny pay cut to move. We were barely making financial ends meet as it was, and my husband was worried about me taking a pay cut. I remember saying to him,

"I promise you, within a year, I will move up, and I know I will be able to make more money than I could have if I were to stay at the credit union." And I did! The company was a wonderful place for me with amazing leaders, mentors, and sponsors who allowed me the flexibility to be a mom and to finish my bachelor's degree. I followed the same philosophy of constantly learning new things and moving in multiple positions to understand all parts of the business but still never realized that sales was an option for me to explore in my career path.

Shortly after earning my bachelor's degree, I was interviewing for a promotion. My company had just gone through a merger, and there was a mix of senior level leaders all learning how to work and partner together. I had an interview with one of these new leaders from the acquired company. I came highly recommended by my current leadership team, and I was excited for the interview and to meet someone from the new company. I was always eager to learn. At the beginning of the interview, his first comment was a scoff at my degree and from where I received it. He was fortunate enough to have attended a high-profile east coast school that had a leading business degree program, which he proudly taunted. I had, however, earned a liberal arts degree from a local hometown university. Within an instant, I forgot about all my hard work of raising a family, working fulltime while attending school fulltime, and graduating summa cum laude. I was immediately mentally transported back to seven years earlier to my high school vice principal's office with feelings of me never amounting to anything. Needless to say, I didn't get that promotion. However, this incident triggered in me a reaction: I never wanted to feel this sense of powerlessness again. Within a couple of weeks, I was taking the Graduate Management Admission Test (GMAT) and applying to MBA programs.

My career continued to take off, and I continued to advance while completing my MBA. Balancing being a mom, a career professional, and a student had become a normal way of life, which is why once

I graduated, I wanted to continue to be in school, but this time, I wanted to teach and help other adults reach their dreams. While continuing to work fulltime, I applied to be an adjunct professor and was excited when I was accepted as a member of the faculty. My ability to take on new positions and tackle the hard business challenges had taught me so many lessons that I now had a forum to share these lessons with others. For six years, I continued to grow and learn with my students while working fulltime. My favorite part was when a student would come to me with a real-world business problem, and we would solve it together in class. Seeing their eyes light up when they figured something out together was thrilling. I have many examples where, together with a student, we developed a strategy to effectively communicate an idea to an executive or to learn how to partner with a difficult co-worker. Regardless of the outcome, the value of the process in coming up with various solutions was where the real learning took place and resulted in lessons they could carry forward to help them further their careers. I realized these strategies are the same strategies that I could use to help other companies as well, so taking my next step was just around the corner. It was a busy and full life but not yet truly fulfilled. My next adventure was to be in sales.

What motivated you to be in sales versus any other career?

I, like so many other women, fell into sales. My son was getting ready to graduate from high school, and it was now my time to look for my next career move. I was ready to move from my consistent and safe company that provided security for my family and that allowed me to have the balance of being a leader and a mom to something a bit more challenging. I felt God tugging on my heart, telling me it was the right time for a change and that I was ready to continue to grow and move ahead.

I began to apply and interview with various companies. I was in my third-round interview with a tech company and was meeting with the COO to be their head of corporate training. I was excited for a role where I could combine my passion for teaching with my love for driving operational business improvements and transformation. During the interview, as I explained my strategy to develop a solution to fix their current operational problems and how to lead through the change when the COO leaned back in his chair and said, "You would be fantastic in business development." I was shocked to say the least! And to be completely honest, I didn't know exactly what he meant by "business development" as I had spent the last fourteen years of my career on the consumer support side of the business. I thought to myself, "He couldn't be talking about business sales ... that's not me." Quickly thinking on my feet, I replied, "I have spent most of my career trying to sell new ideas and make changes throughout the company, so I guess you could say I've always been in that sort of role." We continued with the interview, but that comment stuck with me over the next few days.

I started to research business development roles and reached out to a few peers in the industry. The feedback I kept getting was overwhelming, that moving into B2B sales would be a great second career. My background of consistently tackling the hard jobs to turn around organizations, solving unique business challenges, and partnering with various organizations to reach common goals could easily transition into understanding client issues, providing business solutions to solve problems, and negotiating contractual agreements. I would have never made the connection, but others did and were actually shocked I hadn't considered it before. Learning more about these business development roles and seeing them connect the dots began to give me the confidence that I could really be successful in a sales role. Within a month I had a couple job offers, and after much prayer and reflection, I took the leap, having the same conversation with my husband I had had fifteen years earlier: "Please just trust me. This is the right move!" Wow! Never in my wildest dreams would I have known I would be more financially stable and fulfilled in my career. Being recognized my first year as a top performer and consistently meeting that expectation every year along with the personal comments from my clients demonstrate to me every day that I made the right move. My only regret was not recognizing this sooner!

What is one or more myths or negative perceptions about sales or women in sales that need dispelling?

When I finally decided to make the leap in sales, I was excited. Albeit a little bit nervous, I felt confident in my decision. In my last few weeks while transitioning my responsibilities before switching companies, my current boss questioned my decision. He said—and I quote—"You are NOT a salesperson. You don't have the right personality." He was right in one aspect. I was not the big personality or a flashy salesperson that I had always associated with salespeople. I wasn't a schmoozer, a social butterfly, or a "let's make a deal" type of personality. I was the thinker, quiet and reserved in my approach—more introverted and shy. I was a person who was driven to finding the right solutions to problems, validating the data, and never boasting or taking credit for the outcome. Yet, I was definitely not passive. I didn't avoid conflict at all, and I was passionate, challenging the status quo, constantly asking "How come?" or suggesting "Why not?" My outspoken and Socratic questioning approach to try to solve things differently earned me the feedback early in my career of being "too intimidating" to higher executives. I could never sit by and accept mediocre results or watch someone stay with the status quo when there was a better solution. In his mind and the minds of so many others, that didn't fit the typical sales executive profile of being fun and agreeable.

Unlike so many times before when I felt discouraged, I did not let his comment shake me or influence my decision to leave. I had succeeded in my role with him, winning many awards and recognition. I appreciated his attempt to try to retain me, but discouraging me in my new adventure wouldn't work. With God's guidance, I was confident in my decision. This decision was 100% about me and not my former boss. Plus, I knew something he didn't—that, in fact, I had been selling my ideas and concepts my entire career. Sales is not a cookie cutter personality mold. People in sales have various styles and approaches, but the successful ones have the ability to drive solutions that solve their clients' problems. That is what is important, not their personality type. Yes, I am a "fixer" by nature. If there is a problem, I assess, evaluate, crunch data, and create a solution ... But isn't that sales in its most natural sense? Finding the right solution for clients and developing a strategy together is my passion and, frankly, why I have been so successful in sales. Someone doesn't need to be pushy or loud to get things done; sometimes a quiet, thoughtful approach that has a clear strategy and a return on investment wins the deal.

What advice would you give to a young woman (or your 19-year-old self) who is considering a career in sales? What can anyone of any age do right now to prepare for a career in sales?

Tip 1: Never doubt yourself.

Do not assume that someone older and wiser or someone with more experience is right. Don't assume that your background or where you came from reflects who you are or where you are going. As Ursula Burns, former CEO of Xerox used to say, "Where you are is not who you are." Neither of my parents ever graduated high school, but that never stopped them or me from pushing forward, knowing I could do more. I did not have any knowledge or background in sales, but I used all my previous experience to bridge that gap and did not doubt my abilities.

I remember in my first few months in sales, I was constantly thinking, "Should I say this?" or "Should I mention that?" Then later, I would privately mention my idea or thought to someone, and they would question why I didn't say it early. I was suffering from imposter syndrome, thinking none of my knowledge and business experience mattered because I was new in sales. But I quickly pivoted when I stepped back and started simply realizing how I will be successful in sales, that my "fixer" mentality is my superpower.

Women constantly face the challenge of how to balance work and family. I was constantly told I couldn't balance everything. I will be the first to admit my life is messy and not perfect, and everyone's view on work-life balance is different. But I do know both my children, now adults, carefully watched me through our journey and are my biggest fans while I am theirs. Everyone is different, and it is those differences that make us special. This is important to remember because those people who are trying to impose their beliefs deemed to be fact are facts for only them. Make your own path that is right for you.

Tip 2: Have faith! If there is an opportunity, JUMP!

Trust your gut. I have always felt when my gut is telling me something good or bad, it is actually a sign from God. I have faith not only in Him but also in myself to understand discernment—whether it is a big move like changing jobs or a small one like "Should I follow back up with that customer one more time?" When I have failed to trust my gut, I failed! It has always come to haunt me and, over and over again, to always trust my gut and have faith.

There are multiple opportunities you will come by in life. My advice is always to JUMP! It could be to jump head-on and face your fears; trust your gut and take that leap. If it is truly what you want, it will work out. Or your gut might be telling you to jump back—avoid the freight train coming down those tracks and make the decision to not go forward. Either way it is FANTASTIC because it was your choice. Know that whatever path you take, it is right, and you will figure out how to navigate it.

As I made the final decision to move into sales, my mentor told me "The only regret you are going to have is not making the change sooner." He was so right!! I could have moved into sales sooner; it would have been financially better, and I know now that I could have juggled my career and home. If only I had known!

Tip 3: LEARN LEARN LEARN!! Be a lifelong learner.

To prepare for a job in sales, you need to really learn first about yourself.

What are your strengths, your unique qualities? There is no one-size-fits-all in sales. But accurately and honestly discovering your personal strengths and knowing what are more of your watch-out areas is extremely important. It is all about trying to understand what you bring to the table and partnering with those who bring in other qualities. For example, in a business sales meeting, I try to balance the approach and strategy of presenters to make sure there is a natural flow that will match directly with the client. I cannot be everything to everyone, and I accept that. But I know my history and talents I bring to the table can be valuable, too.

What motivates you and excites you? If you are motivated and excited, your clients will be, too. Your motivation is important to figure out if you are going to go into sales because next is what should you sell? Too often, we choose a path we think we will be good at but then do not find the right job/or company that brings the passion that drove us in our first decision.

Next, always be learning about the people, the processes, and the products as well as the industries and companies you work with every day.

- Do the work and learn about your clients and how you can help them.

- Learn about your own company and how things get done. Sales is not a one-person job but requires the help of others and eventually the operations to support what you sell. Understand what is needed to make all parts successful.

- Learn new approaches and other styles in all interactions. See the value others bring to the table. Whether it is interacting with a CEO or a front-line new hire, you can learn something interesting and insightful. You can also learn what you don't like or how not to act; that could be just as valuable.

- Find a great mentor and a sponsor. A mentor is someone who can guide you, challenge you, and help you with new ideas and approaches. A sponsor is someone in your corner, who believes in you and who will help you navigate your career and advocate on your behalf. And, when you reach a place in leadership, please become someone else's mentor or sponsor.

And, finally, have fun! Preparing for a career in sales can be the best time of your life. Getting to go to work every day and use the gifts God gave you to help impact the world—that is amazing. How can sales impact the world? Well, I help companies solve business problems; these companies help people every day get new homes, cars, health insurance, medical care, and much more. In addition, I help create thousands of jobs around the world; some of those jobs are filled by young moms just like I was starting out in an entry-level company.

Biography

Ginnette is an avid problem-solver and has gravitated towards creative solutions focused on delivering profitable results, which led her to an exciting second career as a global executive in business development. She is passionate about change management and has used her advocacy in leadership at well-respected organizations to include a corporation that sells print and digital services and products, a multinational technology corporation, a telecommunications company, and now an omnichannel business transformation company. She believes there is always a better way and used this philosophy to spearhead her graduate studies and eventually her role as an adjunct professor in business, leadership management, and CAPSTONE classes for bachelor's and master's studies. She is the proud wife and mom of two humans, a dog, and a cat. You can find her hiking outdoors, reading a great book, and drinking coffee!

TAKE A CHANCE ON YOURSELF NOW

Leslie Venetz
Founder

What was your path to the sales industry?

I knew I wanted a career where I could help others; I never thought it would be sales. When I realized that I needed a job where I could do good and also pay my bills, I stumbled into sales as a profession.

With a background in policy debate and Model United Nations, sales came easily to me.

That's not to say that sales is easy, but I was able to leverage those existing rhetoric skills to experience early success.

I felt empowered by a job that required creativity and grit. I was motivated by controlling my own paycheck. After only two months in my first sales role, I knew that a career in sales was "it" for me.

Looking back, I can hardly believe that an entry-level sales role cold calling C-suite executives at the rate of 100+ dials a day endeared me to the profession. But I was good at it—really good at it.

What motivated you to be in sales versus any other career?

Frankly, I wasn't motivated to be in sales.

Sales was not a profession that anybody talked about as an exciting or respected career choice. Sales felt like a catch-all phrase for anybody who had a job where they tricked you into buying something you didn't need.

I took my first sales job because I thought it would be a cool company to work for, and the only open position happened to be in sales.

It's a good thing I did. Sales is my calling. I am a proud sales professional.

I wish that kids were taught about the opportunities available in B2B sales. It's a job that shouldn't (and often doesn't) require a college degree. It is a path to reducing the generational wealth gap. Buying and selling is an essential part of anybody's life.

The reality is that everybody is selling something; they just might not recognize it yet!

For future generations, I hope when asked "What motivated you to be in sales?" they will talk about women like those featured in this book. They will share a story about an amazing buying process they experienced and how it made them realize they enjoy helping others make informed buying decisions.

I hope, in the future, that women are motivated to be in sales in significantly greater numbers than we see today. And I hope that when they get there, we've laid the foundation for their inclusion and success.

What is one or more myths or negative perceptions about sales or women in sales that need dispelling?

I could share a much longer list of the most harmful myths I've heard sales leaders and hiring managers repeat, but here are five I hear most often.

1. Women aren't attracted to a career in sales; that's actually why there is a gender diversity problem.
2. Women aren't tough enough to get the job done so they won't be successful. Sales is a man's game.
3. Sales *is* an inclusive environment. Women *are* welcomed and supported. The experiences of discrimination that you've encountered are an exception.

   The number of myths that are based on a complete void of understanding what gender discrimination looks like in practice is quite damaging. As damaging as the outright "women don't even want to be in sales" myths are, a new narrative that sales is already an inclusive place and that our work is done is just as harmful.
4. The best way to sell is the way that we've been selling—the timeless "if it's not broken, don't fix it" philosophy.

   The issue is that those historical perspectives and processes happen to be predominantly based on the lived experience of the cishet White male. There are many ways to sell.

   It's essential that our sales teams better represent how our buyers want to buy, which means there are as many ways to sell as there are ways to buy.

   And I'll wrap it up with a personal favorite:
5. Women ruin the vibe on the sales floor. It was more fun before we had to be PC.

What advice would you give to a young woman (or your 19-year-old self) who is considering a career in sales? What can anyone of any age do right now to prepare for a career in sales?

Do it.

Sales is a rewarding profession. It is challenging, mentally stimulating, profitable, and fun.

Have an extremely keen eye when selecting which sales organization to join. Talk in-depth about their culture, leadership philosophy, actions behind their inclusion agenda, etcetera.

I've seen former teachers, restaurant staff, warehouse workers, and others successfully transition to careers in sales. Sales is a job where anybody with soft skills, a bit of gusto, and a good amount of grit can thrive.

Take a chance on yourself now.

Sales development representative (SDR) roles start at an annual salary of $50,000 to $70,000 with skilled SDRs topping the six-figure mark with only two to three years of experience.

Find the right organization that is happy to train you and that will continue to invest in your growth. Once you find it, accept your first sales job today.

No profession is perfect. You may face more dark moments in sales than in other professions, but I am sure you will also achieve incredible highs. Your voice matters. You matter. Join us.

Biography

Leslie Venetz has spent her career in B2B sales. In 2018, she founded Sales Team Builder, a sales consultancy that supports 0- to 50-person B2B sales teams who want to create buyer-centric processes and mindsets.

Leslie is passionate about making sales a more inclusive, respected profession. She connects with and inspires the next generation of sales professionals on SalesTipsTok, her channel on a video social networking app.

When Leslie is not selling or talking about sales, you can find her on a SoulCycle bike, reading, cooking, planning her next vacation, or spending time with family in her home state of Montana.

ABOUT THE COMPILER

Heidi Solomon-Orlick is a Business Process Outsourcing (BPO) industry veteran with more than thirty years of business-to-business (B2B) consultative sales and executive leadership experience. Throughout her illustrious sales career, Heidi has managed a portfolio of contracts valued in excess of $1 billion and has created thousands of jobs around the globe.

As a professional in the male-dominated world of B2B sales, Heidi has dedicated a large part of her career to nurturing and mentoring women in sales and sales management. She recognized the significant gender inequity in professional sales and became even more determined to help democratize the industry and position sales as a viable career choice for young women.

To that end, Heidi founded and is the CEO of GirlzWhoSell LLC and currently serves as board President of the GirlzWhoSell Empowerment Fund (GWSEF) nonprofit. The mission of GirlzWhoSell is to close the gender gap in professional sales and build the largest pipeline of diverse, early-stage female sales talent throughout the world. GirlzWhoSell provides training, mentoring, career consulting, and placement for college and high school aged women interested in pursuing a career in B2B sales. The focus of the GWSEF nonprofit is to provide the much-needed educational funding and scholarships for women from under-served and under-represented communities who want to explore sales as a career option. In 2021, GirlzWhoSell was a finalist and recognized as first runner-up for the 2021 Best New Business of the Year Award through Women in Business Club. GirlzWhoSell is more than a company; it is a movement.

In 2021, Heidi was awarded two gold Stevie awards for Women of the Year in Sales and Worldwide Sales Executive of the Year. She was inducted into the Top 50 Women by Top 100 Magazine and was published as a first-time author in the book *Upward: Leadership Lessons for Women on the Rise*. Heidi hosts the GirlzWhoSell Spotlight Podcast and is a sought-after industry keynote speaker, panelist, and moderator. She recently served as an advisory board member for the Stevie Awards Women Future Conference and has been a multi-year judge for the Stevie Women in Business Awards.

Heidi is a fierce advocate for diversity, equity, and inclusion. She sits on the Modern Sales Pros and LeadsCouncil DE&I Committees and previously served as a co-chair of the International Association of Outsourcing Professionals (IAOP) Women's Empowerment, Leadership, and Diversity Chapter. She is an active venture capital investor in women and minority-owned businesses that are making a positive impact on the world.

Heidi lives in Henniker, New Hampshire with her husband and soul mate of twenty-seven years, David Orlick; their two cats, Bones and Linus; and their adorable dog, Revis, who definitely runs the family. She is the mother of three amazing boys who are the center of her universe.

Made in the USA
Middletown, DE
18 February 2022